D0432243

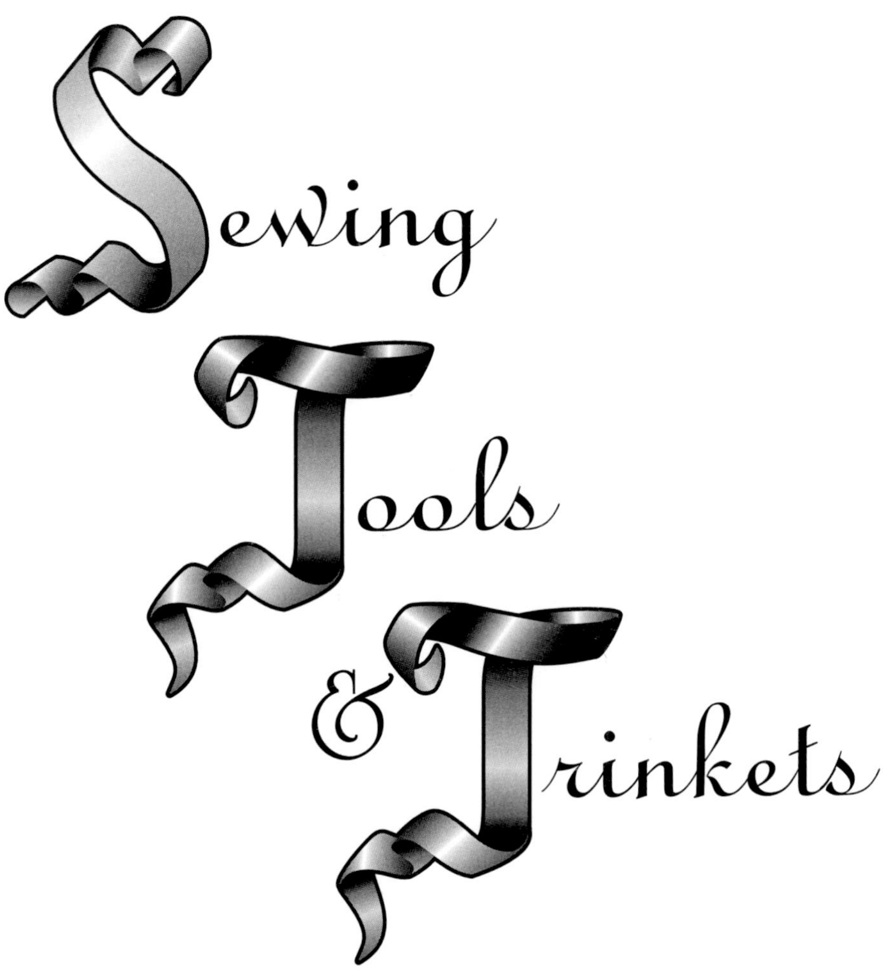

Sewing Tools & Trinkets

Collector's Identification & Value Guide

Helen Lester Thompson

COLLECTOR BOOKS

A Division of Schroeder Publishing Co., Inc.

The current values in this book should be used only as a guide. They are not intended to set prices, which vary from one section of the country to another. Auction prices as well as dealer prices vary greatly and are affected by condition as well as demand. Neither the author nor the publisher assumes responsibility for any losses that might be incurred as a result of consulting this guide.

Cover design: Beth Summers
Book design: Sherry Kraus

Searching for a Publisher?

We are always looking for knowledgeable people considered to be experts within their fields. If you feel that there is a real need for a book on your collectible subject and have a large comprehensive collection, contact Collector Books.

COLLECTOR BOOKS
P.O. Box 3009
Paducah, Kentucky 42002–3009

www.collectorbooks.com

Contents

Dedication

To friends that inspire the joy of learning and sharing, Paul Pilgrim and Gerald Roy.

Acknowledgments

The diversity and quality of the items representing needlework from the eighteenth century to the late twentieth century that appear in this book are through the generosity of the following collectors. Those who had one item to lend contributed no less than those with many items. There are many pieces to the puzzle yet to be filled and all of the collectors added new pieces. My sincere appreciation to each one.

Faye Beckwith
Jeannie Helen Chryn
Connie Collis
Lois DeLuca
Debra Fuller
George Gaydos
Mollie Heron
Mary Jo Holmes
Betty Hoopes
Glendora Hutson
Joyce Knapp
Lynn Loyd
Pam Osborne
Pegasus
Paul Pilgrim
Gerald Roy
Meredith Schroeder
Kathlyn Sullivan
Miriam Tuska

Credits:

Photography of book cover and chapter introductions: Richard Walker

Photography of collections and sewing machines, Chryn Collection of new thimbles: Richard Walker

Photography of groupings with the chapter headings: Charley Lynch

Book design by: Sherry Kraus

Cover design by: Beth Summers

Introduction

Although many sewing tool pieces have been acquired by collectors and sewing enthusiasts, there are many more out there, waiting to be found and incorporated into the history of needlework and sewing tools. This book was compiled to assist in the search for these tools and trinkets, to serve as a reference for the growing number of people interested in this area of arts and crafts.

As I gathered the tools for photographing and researched their history, I realized that there are limited sources of information available. In this age of computers and Internet access, this will undoubtedly change, but in the meantime, museum collections

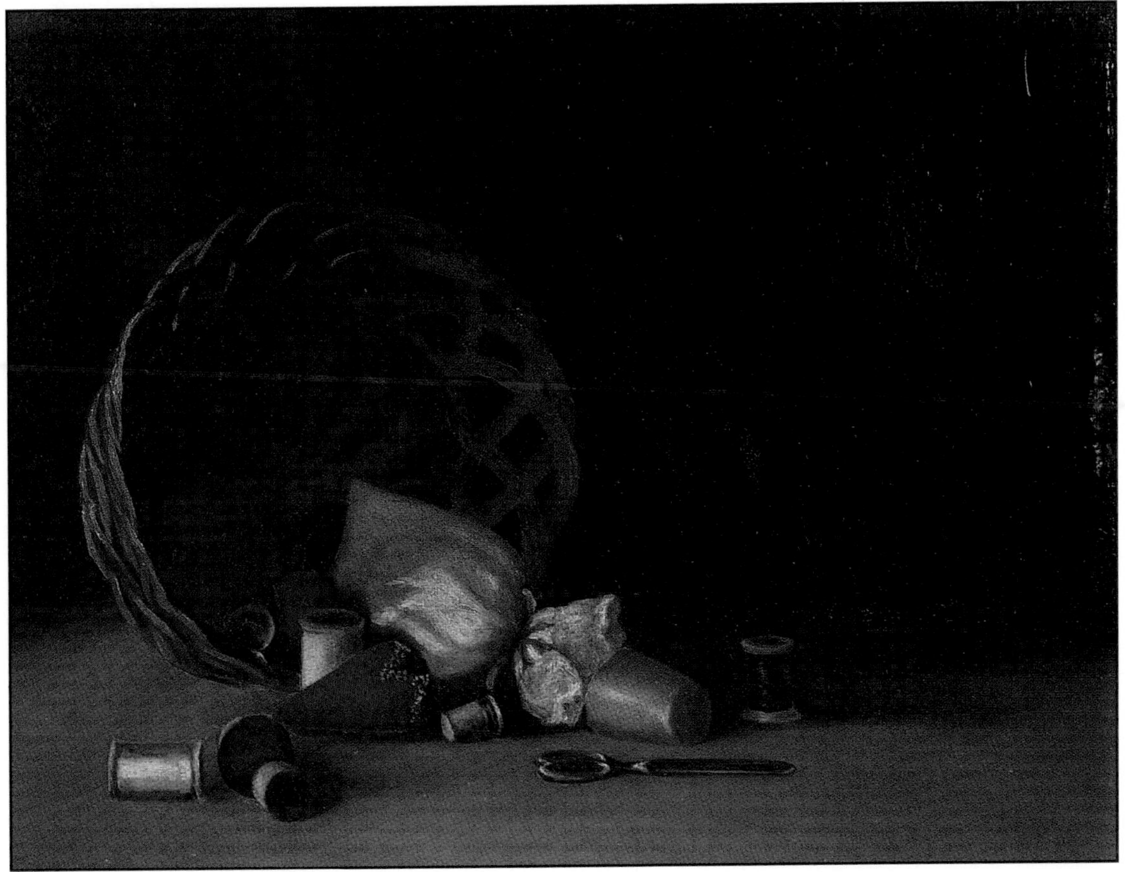

Still life. G. Reed, American, late nineteenth century. Oil on stretched canvas. This painting is in the style of the Dutch Masters. The willow basket contents include spools of cotton and silk thread, silver cap strawberry emery, scissors, silver thimble, cotton sewing bag, and red ball of yarn. Courtesy of Glendora Hutson.

remain a valuable resource. Excavations throughout the world have provided evidence of the sorts of sewing tools that have existed, showing us what they were made of and how they were used. As you travel, make use of these historical collections; take the opportunity to view the artifacts and transform them into a living, functional history.

Historical context is especially exciting when one comes across the unexpected find, such as a pin ball, a German chatelaine or a Swedish handmade clamp. Through these artifacts and learning about the development of bronze, iron, and steel comes a realization of just how young our country is relation to the rest of the world. The contribution of these "ancient" tools to the history of weaving, embroidery, and lace-making is immeasurable and the fact that they have survived to delight us in the twenty-first century is a true miracle. Of course, Native American cultures were accomplished as basket makers, weavers, and potters, but as is the case in many very early cultures, examples of their tools have disappeared, either worn out from use or lost in the sands of time.

In viewing numerous individual collections for this project, I was given an educational opportunity that afforded me great excitement and pleasure. As you develop your own collection, it is important to incorporate education into your pursuit. Gerald Roy, in his lecture "Buying and Collecting," suggests that dedication and commitment to your interest through research and scholarship are important. Factors such as condition of the item, materials of construction, availability/unavailability, and how one item relates to another are critical in determining provenance and, ultimately, value. There are responsibilities as a collector that include preservation versus restoration and sharing of knowledge, as well as collected treasures. Your own enthusiasm, expertise, and generosity can contribute to a quality experience for all collectors.

CUBE
QUEEN VICTORIA
SILVER EY'D
SHARPS
39
WARRANTED

Chapter One

Pins and Needles

The straight pin was primitive, rare, and expensive until the mid-nineteenth century, when English manufacturers refined the quality and developed the one-piece straight pin. The lower cost of pins was the result of lower steel prices and mass production. Although French pins never dominated the world market, they were sought after because of their high quality and desirability as a clothing fastener. According to information available, the straight pin is still used as a clothing fastener by very conservative Amish sects.

The various pincushions that became available resulted from the low cost of pins and the styles of the period. Although the small pin holders of the past continued to be used, Victorian pincushions took off in form and materials of construction. They were ivory, vegetable ivory, glass, celluloid, wood, leather, and fabric. The cushions were often fashion statements made of fabrics, decorative work, and colors of the period. The top photograph on page 13 is an example of one of the more decorative handmade pincushions, with its crocheted silver thread overlay, lovely silk rose, border of leaves, sawdust, sand, horsehair, and wool fibers. Because rust was a problem with iron pins, small closed containers were often used. An abrasive material, such as emery, kept points sharpened and scraped off the rust. Emery was the material of choice, if available. The diverse and handy three-layer pin holder has many names: disc pincushion, pin pocket book, sandwich pincushion, pinsafe, pin-keep, or pinwheel (see pages 11 and 18). This style of pin holder became popular with businesses as a means of advertisement, either for sale or as a give-away.

Archaeological finds in Europe and other parts of the world date needle-like tools as far back as 20,000 years ago. A number of museums have examples of Bronze Age and Iron Age needles in their collections. By the fourteenth century, the steel needle had come to Europe from the Eastern steelmaking centers of Antioch, Andrianople, and Damascus. By the sixteenth century due to Moorish influences, Italy and Spain became steelmaking centers and continued in this fashion until the nineteenth century when England and Germany began to dominate the world market.

Needle holders of earlier periods were small and simple in design. It was not until the mid-nineteenth century when steel needles became affordable and readily available that the holders expanded in size and design. The French developed three different kinds and sizes of needles for use with differing threads, from coarse string to fine silk, and holders were developed to meet these circumstances. They, like pincushions, became affordable and available and were made out of a variety of materials from paper to gold. Many unusual and clever figural holders were made in various countries, all reflecting their culture in design and materials (see page 26).

1st row:

1. England; horn pincushion stand, original pincushions with worn nap; c. 1850, $150.00.
2. USA; Victorian fashion half-doll pincushion; the doll is the head and breast plate of a full doll made of papier-mâché; c. 1870, $250.00.

2nd row:

1. England; pin ball (pincushion); silver band with ring; filled with a fiber; early silk covered pin balls often had needle work coverings and were dated; c. 1800, $200.00.
2. Spain; wood shoe with brass trim, inscription "la Boule," velvet cushion; 3½"; c. 1880, $25.00.
3. England; pin ball (pincushion); velvet cover with silver ring around the center with initials "PBR"; cotton label basted on ball "pincushion made and used by Polly Brown Ricaida Laus 1805"; $250.00 – 350.00.

1st row:

1. England; sitting duck; nickel plate, velvet cushion; 3½"; c. 1900, $80.00.
2. Germany; walking bear; carved wood, wool cushion; 4"; c. 1900, $100.00.
3. England; rhinoceros; pot metal, velvet cushion; 4"; c. 1880, $125.00.

2nd row:

1. England; pig; silver plate, saddle with flower designs, velvet cushion; 2½"; c. 1900, $85.00.
2. England; seated camel; nickel plate over pot metal, souvenir shield "Prospect Point," Niagara," velvet cushion; 3"; c. 1880, $100.00.
3. England; pig; brass, brush-work finish, velvet cushion; 3"; c. 1900, $90.00.

3rd row:

1. England; bird; pot metal, silver finish rubbed off, velvet cushion; c. 1890, $65.00.
2. England; elephant; polished metal, cotton cushion, raised trunk; 2½"; c. 1900, $60.00.
3. England; fox; hallmark "London, sterling, 1892," velvet cushion; 2"; $150.00.
4. England; elephant; pot metal, velvet cushion; 2"; c. 1900, $55.00.

4th row:

1. England; snail; sterling, velvet cushion; 1"; c. 1900, $90.00.
2. England; pig; sterling, velvet cushion; 1"; c. 1900, $100.00.
3. England; rodent; pot metal, velvet cushion; 1½"; c. 1800, $55.00.

1st row:
1. USA; pincushion; bisque doll, wrist ribbon; 2"; c. 1915, $65.00.
2. India; pincushion; damascene style brass with an unusual stand; 2"; c. 1915, $40.00.
3. USA; hoof; velvet cushion; 2½" x 3¼"; c. 1910, $75.00.

2nd row:
1., 2. Same as first row #1.
3. England; terrier; bisque, velvet cushion; 1½"; c. 1920, $40.00.

Small doll pincushions, such as these, were sometimes joined with a long silk ribbon and worn around the neck. Bisque doll called "Frozen Charlotte."

1st row:
1. USA; pot metal swan; velvet cushion; 2½" x 3"; c. 1880, $55.00.
2. Asia; pierced ivory pin keep; layers hand sewn together; 1" x 2½"; c. 1860, $90.00.
3. England; English Bulldog in uniform at attention; nickel-plated pot metal, cushion on its back; 2" x 2½"; c. 1875, $75.00.
4. England; gilt finish cornucopia; decorative guitar and lute showing, and showing mandolin on the back; woven silk brocade cushion; 3½" x 2½"; c. 1875, $75.00.

1st row:

1. USA; hand made of silk fabric and silk embroidery thread, chain stitch loop for thimble, black glass buttons decorate both centers; 3½"; c. 1915, $10.00.
2. England; wood platform with worn velvet cushion, handmade braid edging, legs of horn; 4½" x 4½"; c. 1875, $50.00.
3. USA; sweet grass basket woven by Native Americans, New York State, often cushions were added by individuals or businesses that purchased the basket; 3½" x 3"; c. 1900, $65.00.

2nd row:

1. Same as #3 in 1st row; 2" x 2"; c. 1900, $45.00.
2. England; toilet pins, Abel Morrall's, glass heads, paper cube; c. 1885, $25.00.
3. England; pin keep, tartan ware with decal of Robert Burns statue; 2"; c. 1875, $120.00.

1st row:

1. USA; Bluejay on a limb; embellished with flowers, pincushion in knot hole, celluloid; c. 1930, $45.00.
2. England; pin box, embossed leather, inside top silk faille for needles, lid attached along back; 2¼" x 3½"; c. 1875, $30.00 – 45.00.

2nd row:

1. England, wood transfer ware, scene "Saratoga Monument, Schuyerville, N.Y.," shield-style with blue velvet; c. 1875, $110.00.
2. England; pin safe, wood transfer ware, heart shape, scene "state capitol, Albany, NY"; c. 1865, $110.00.
3. England; decorative pin cushion; dome shape, silver thread crocheted medallion overlay on silk, handmade, silk flowers and leaf embellishment, good condition; 2½" x 2"; c. 1865, $65.00.

Pincushions; English hallmark, Gorham; c. 1875, $75.00 – 90.00.

1. Sunflower; black velvet cushion; 4".
2. Shoe; red velvet cushion; 3½" x 2".

England; pincushions, horn, holes drilled for brass thread shoe laces; 3" x 5"; c. 1860, $90.00.

1st row:

1. Asia; chair; ivory and vegetable ivory; c. 1875, $45.00.
2. Asia; three tiers, ivory and vegetable ivory; c. 1875, $50.00.
3. England; walnut base with pieced cushion; c. 1880, $75.00.
4. England; walnut base, silk cushion; c. 1880, $35.00.

2nd row:

1., 2. Asia; vegetable ivory, hand carved; c. 1890, $30.00.
3., 4. England; bone, hand carved; c. 1890, $45.00.
5. Asia; ivory, hand carved, hand painted; c. 1880, $65.00
6. China; painted china head, silk cushion; c. 1880, $35.00.

3rd row:

1. USA; Tomato emery; wool fabric and felt top; c. 1910, $10.00.
2., 3. USA; Shaker style woven baskets; velvet cushions; c. 1880, $40.00.
4., 5. England; tunbridge wood; c. 1860, $110.00.
   5. double ended pincushion; $100.00
6. USA; emery; embroidered top; c. 1910, $10.00.

4th row:

1. – 5. Japan; emeries; c. 1915, $10.00 – 15.00.
6. USA; emery, sterling cap, Unger Bros.; c. 1900, $140.00.
7., 8. Japan; emeries; c. 1915, $10.00 – 20.00.
9. Japan; carrot emery; c. 1915, $5.00.

1st row:

1. Turkey; slipper; leather with braid trim; c. 1890, $40.00.
2. USA; lady's shoe; burnished pot metal; marked "People's Outfitting Co., the store that saves you money"; c. 1900, $50.00.
3. England; slipper; celluloid covered paper, joined with over-cast embroidery; c. 1890, $25.00.

2nd row:

1. USA; lady's shoe; nickel finish pot metal, marked "Washington, DC the Capitol," "JB515"; c. 1900, $35.00.
2. Man's shoe; "made in Japan," polished metal; c. 1919, $40.00.
3. Yugoslavia; slipper; leather with braid trim; c. 1890, $20.00.

3rd row:

1. England; slipper; sterling; 1⅛"; c. 1900, $75.00.
2. Lady's slipper; "made in Occupied Japan," metal, feather, and shell designs; c. 1937, $35.00.
3. USA; lady's shoe; polished metal; c. 1900, $30.00.
4. USA; lady's shoe; copperwash metal; c. 1920, $40.00.

4th row:

1. Birmingham, England; shoe (Dutch-style); sterling; 1906, $80.00.
2. USA; lady's boot; brass; c. 1910, $40.00.
3. England; slipper; wood, hand painted and varnished; pin-cushion and toe holds a thimble; c. 1890, $50.00.

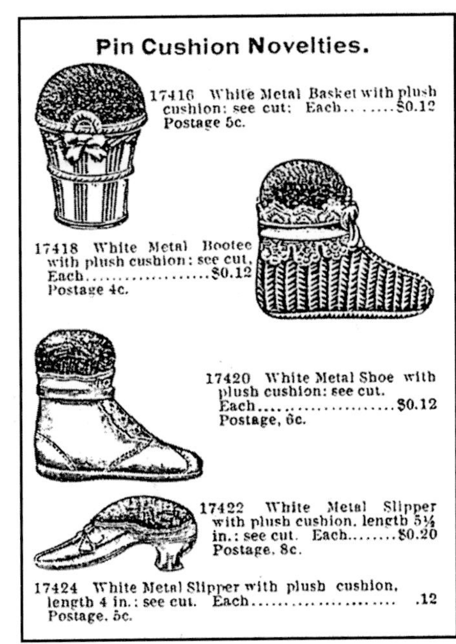

Montgomery Ward ad, 1894 – 1895.

Pin Cushions

1st row:

1. Pennsylvania; needlepoint, medallion design, wool, borders: "Home Sweet," "Home," "Susie," "Walker," back: cotton sateen, basket of flowers fine embroidery; c. 1900, $65.00.
2. Pennsylvania; 4-Patch, hand pieced, silk ribbon, bows attached at corners, maroon linen on back; 8" square; c. 1880, $40.00.

3a. England; casket shape, mahogany, 6¼" x 4" x 2½"; c. 1850, $110.00.
3b. England; handmade, woven fabric, lace trim; 3¼" x 2"; c. 1900, $18.00.

2nd row:

1. USA; velvet with amber glass beads, green felt leaves, emery; 5½"; c. 1900, $60.00.
2. USA; wool felt, flower embroidery and felt leaves, handmade; 3½"; c. 1915, $20.00.

3rd row:

1. USA; silk, pieced, top 1¼" triangles, back rectangles, handmade; 5" square; c. 1890, $35.00.
2. Pennsylvania; pin safe; handmade, wool and silk, wool pages inside, thimble well with sterling, Waite, Thresher Co. thimble; 5½" x 4"; c. 1880, $65.00.
3. Pennsylvania; pins and needles book; handmade, silk fabric, wool pages, silk ribbon tie; 2½" x 3½"; c. 1900, $50.00.

1st row:

1. USA; china pincushion doll; satin and lace; c. 1920, $40.00.
2. Germany; cat and musical pincushion; lace cover; c. 1900, $75.00.
3. USA; boot; Northern Plains Indians, wool with heavy glass beadwork; c. 1890, $45.00.
4. USA; hat; sweet grass, velvet cushion; c. 1900, $20.00.

2nd row:

1. USA; hat; pieced, embroidery embellishment; c. 1890, $30.00.
2. Star; "Niagara Falls, Canada," wool, words and embellishment beadwork; souvenir; c. 1900, $50.00.
3. USA; New Mexico; doll; Navajo, made for Santa Fe Railroad as souvenirs for passengers; c. 1920, $15.00.
4. USA; donut; pieced wool, embroidery, center thimble holder; c. 1890, $15.00.

3rd row:

1. USA; Northern Plains, horn; handmade cotton pincushion; c. 1900, $10.00.
2. Japan; tomato; silk fabric and thread, felt top; c. 1920, $28.00.
3. USA; California Redwood; bucket; souvenir; c. 1920, $20.00.

USA; bird; cotton twill fabric, glass beadwork, under the tail "1898"; $90.00.

1st row:
1. England; needle doll; bisque hand-painted face, hands, feet; stuffed torso, arms, and legs; head and butterfly headdress one piece; jointed doll; silk ribbon, handmade lace front and back; wool pages for needles inside; doll 7"; c. 1880, $150.00.
2. USA; pin safe; floral silk; 10" x 2"; c. 1880, $30.00.
3. England; doll; bisque hand-painted face, hands, shoes, stockings; stuffed torso, arms, and legs, jointed; real hair wig; doll 3¾", needleholder same as #1; c. 1880, $125.00.

2nd row:
Pin Safes
1. Asia; carved ivory with pincushion on top; 1⅞" ; c. 1875, $110.00.
2. England; pressed metal, acorn design moonstone set, back stained wood, silk loop; c. 1875, $75.00.
3. England; mirror with hand-painted paper frame; c. 1890, $60.00.

3rd row:
1. England; hand-carved ivory with hand-painted words and flowers, "Esteem the giver"; 1⅜"; c. 1875, $90.00.
2. Asia; mother of pearl, hand carved, hand sewn; 1½"; c. 1880, $65.00.
3. Asia; carved ivory, hand sewn, hand-painted silk ribbon; 1⅜"; c. 1875, $95.00.

4th row:
1. Great Britian; pin safe; silver plate, top of shield "ARRAS," shield front with facing lions, filigree work; c. 1900, $70.00.
2. Germany; cube; paper, glass head pins, "Best steel toilet pins," Goathead trademark; c. 1880, $15.00.

5th row:
1. USA; mother of pearl, concave pieces, velvet, braid hanger; 1½"; c. 1900, $55.00.
2. Europe; wood covered with assorted shells (both sides), made for export; c. 1890, $65.00.
3. England; Victorian children paper picture; "London Needle Co Pocket Pin Book" on back; c. 1880, $45.00.

1st row:

1. USA; pincushion doll; glazed china, figure holding clown doll, right leg repaired; 5¼"; c. 1920, $50.00.
2. USA; pincushion doll; glazed china, silk; 3½"; c. 1915, $35.00.
3. USA; Liberty Bell; Bicentennial souvenir, signed, glazed pottery; 1976, $5.00.
4. England; 3-D hexagon star; cotton prints, assembly buttonhole embroidery; c. 1910, $55.00.

2nd row:

1 – 3. Lusterware; c. 1930, $25.00 – 40.00.
   1. Japan; elephant.
   2. Japan; terrier dog.
   3. Japan; donkey.

4. USA; bird sitting on whale's tail; blown glass; 3" x 2"; c. 1950, $35.00.

3rd row:

1. England; heart; hand-painted china, velvet; c. 1900, $25.00.
2. Germany; cat; lusterware, velvet; c. 1920, $20.00.
3. USA; pin tray; pressed glass, "see a pin and pick it up, all day long you'll have good luck," C. F. Lange, 513 Franklin Ave.; c. 1900, $85.00.
4. USA; tin box; floral designs and word "PINS" etched; 1½" x 2"; c. 1915, $50.00.

4th row:

1. USA; pin safe; two-sided embroidery; Spinner cottage; c. 1940, $20.00.
2. USA; pin safe; Prudential Insurance Co. Adv.; paper; c. 1920, $20.00.
3. England; pin safe; heart; velvet; handmade; c. 1900, $10.00.

USA; make-do pincushions; Pennsylvania Mennonite, five pieces; c. 1890, $65.00 – 100.00.
1., 2. Flint glass compote, velvet cushions. 3., 4. Flint glass oil lamp base.
5. Pressed glass base, hand-pieced cushion cover.

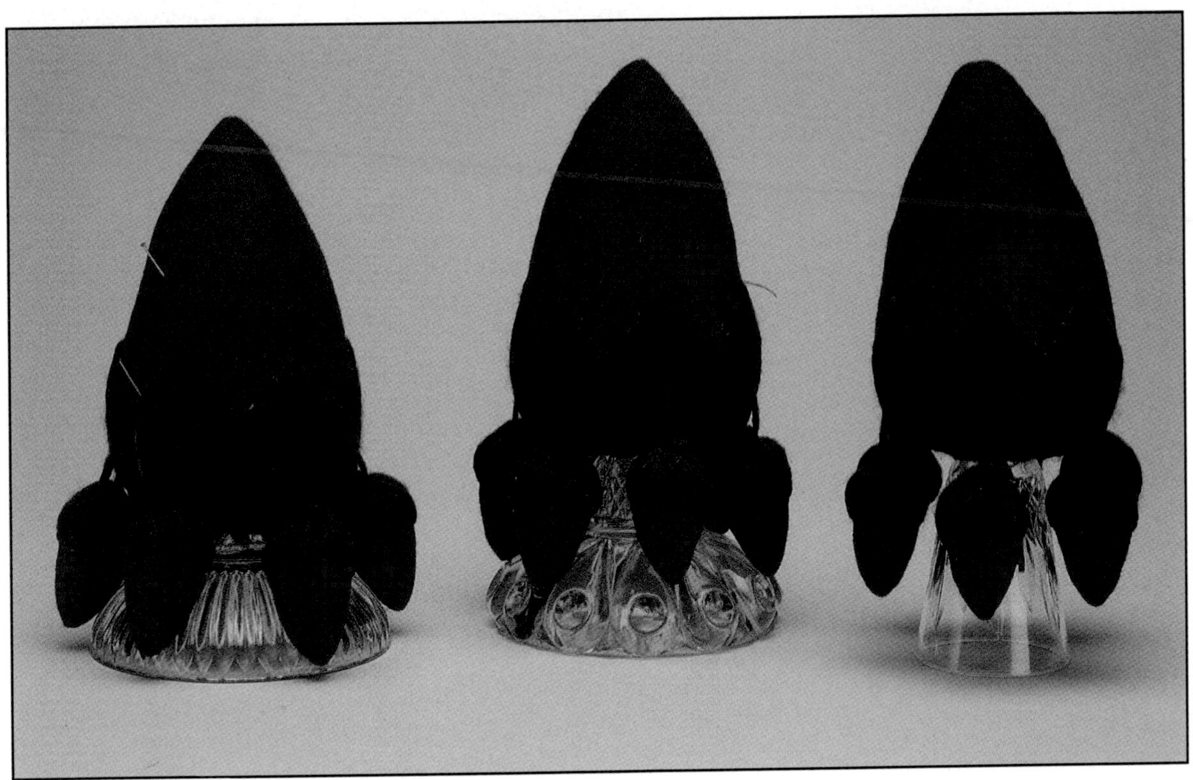

USA; Shipshewana, Indiana; strawberry pincushions, Mennonite; wool fabric and wool yarn, mounted on wine glass and two flint glass compote cups. The base of each pincushion is a recycled item; 8". $125.00 – 170.00.

1st row:
1. England; three-piece set; Staffordshire Enamels, Old Hall copyright drawings Nicola Bayley; 1975, $45.00.
2. China; four dolls; 3" x 6"; c. 1980, $20.00.
3. USA; heart; cotton fabric, stripped piecing; c. 1977, $5.00.

2nd row:
1. USA; cotton crazy patch, machine pieced, sand filled; c. 1980, $7.50.
2. China; three dolls; 1½" x 1½"; c. 1980, $7.50.
3. USA; poodle; metal with gold color finish, thimble holder, tape measure, and pincushion; c. 1950, $10.00.
4. Kentucky, USA; handmade needlepoint, wool yarn, handmade; 1½" x ½". c. 1975; $15.00.

3rd row:
1. USA; apple; metal with gold color finish; c. 1950, $5.00.
2. USA; heart; metal with gold color finish; c. 1950, $5.00.
3. Kentucky, USA; handmade needlepoint, wool yarn, geometric design, 2" x 2". $15.00.

1. USA; pin box; "New Bedford, Mass; quadruple plate, Pairpoint MFG Co, 3720," top: embedded brass safety pin, "A Safe Friend," footed; 1" x 2¼" x 1½"; c. 1880, $100.00.

2. USA; silverplate pin tray, feather and flower designs, used to "catch" straight and safety pins, hair pins and needles; 4" x 2½"; c. 1880, $60.00.

3. Germany; pin holder; dark blue celluloid with decorative silver overlay; c. 1900, $40.00.

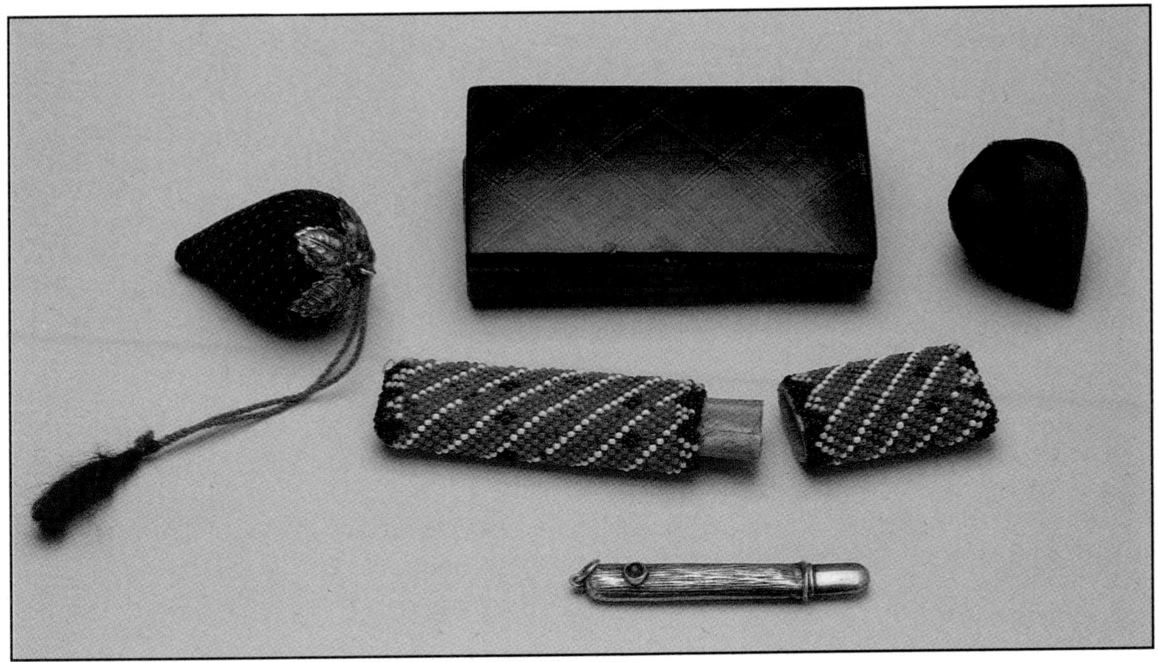

1st row:

1. USA; emery silk cover and tassel; sterling silver leaves as a cap; 1½"; c. 1900, $95.00.
2. England; tartan ware needle book with two wool fabric pages, four silk pockets; marked "Albert" (clan); 1¾" x 2¾"; c. 1875, $175.00.
3. USA; emery, silk cover; velvet leaves; 1¼"; c. 1900, $60.00.

2nd row:

1. USA, New York State; needle holder; bone sheath covered with fine bead work, Native American work; 3" x ⅝" c. 1880, $150.00.

3rd row:

1. USA; needle holder; sterling with decorative stone; 1¾"; c. 1915, $70.00.

Needle cases

1st row:

1. USA; glove darner; sterling, rope-design, larger end darner telescopes on and off for access to needles; c. 1910, $120.00.
2. USA; glove darner; sterling with decorative beading, egg-shaped end telescopes on and off for access to needles; c. 1910, $100.00.

2nd row:

1. USA; sterling open-end needle case; decorative flowers, a chatelaine piece; c. 1910, $75.00.
2. England; bone case covered with mosaic straw; the work has a petit point look, the designs are on both sides and each end; c. 1850, $95.00.
3. England; wood, screw top; c. 1860, $45.00.
4. England; rosewood with bone trim, umbrella shaped; 4½"; c. 1870, $95.00.
5. England; sterling; c. 1890, $80.00.

Sears Roebuck & Co., 1910

No. 8T7261 Fruit Pin Cushion, natural color decorated.

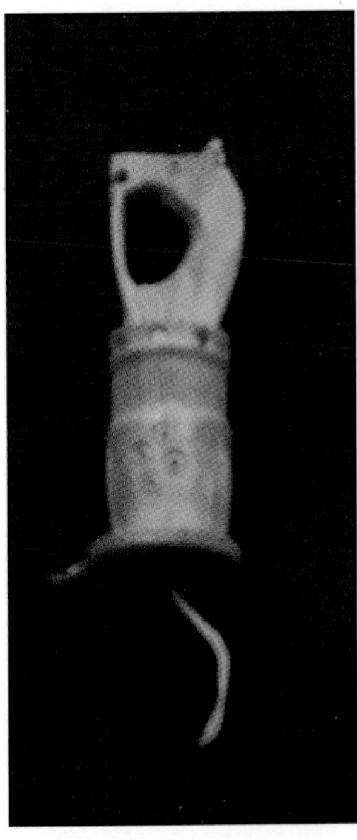

England; needle holder; ivory, hand carved, interior cork liner, horse's head with reins comes out of top; c. 1860, $250.00.

France; needle case; ivory and gold, medallion decoration is an oval glass top covering a wheat shaft design made of light brown hair, gold wire, and seed pearls, 3½"; c. 1860, $600.00.

1st row:

1. USA; paper needle holder; pictorial holiday scene, "The Home Needle Case" ad for Hoyle & Rarick Clo. Co., 606 N. Broadway, St Louis, Mo., the advertising manufactured by Magiuda Novelty Co., New York, N.Y., one packet of Dix and Rand Sharps, seven darning needles; c. 1915, $7.50.
2. Germany; character doll needle holder; painted wood, lift the hat and the needles come to the top, knob at lower right stops the distance the hat can be pulled up; 3⅜"; c. 1910, $80.00.

2nd row:

1. Mexico; obsidian needle from Valley of Mexico; 3"; c. 300 BC, $20.00.

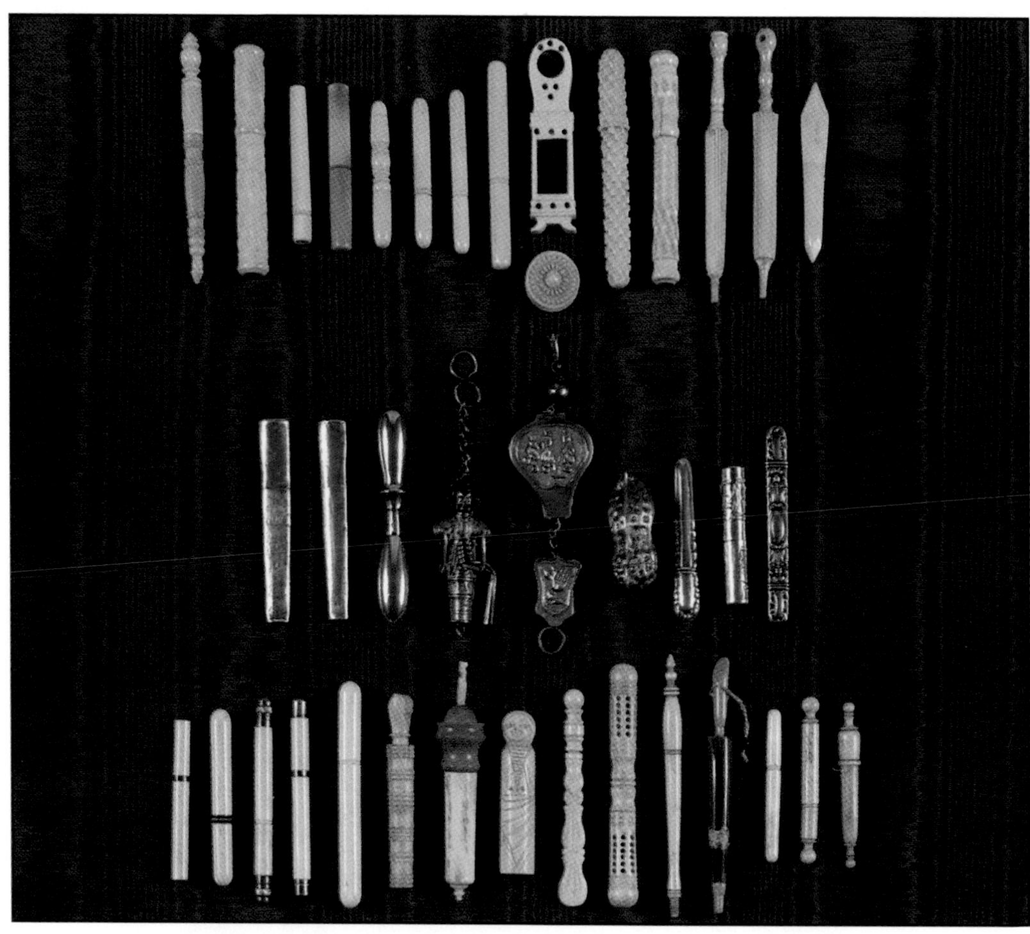

1st row: Asia and England; needle cases; ivory; 1859 – 1880
1., 2., 11., 12. c. 1880, $75.00.
3. – 8. c. 1875 – 1900, $50.00 – 70.00.
9a. Clock-style, pewter and tortoise embellishment; $120.00.
9b. Wax wheel, hand carved, with beeswax; $65.00.
10. English with carved ivory; c. 1860, $75.00.
12., 13. Umbrellas with Stanhope; $80.00 – 120.00.
14. English ivory; c. 1875; $75.00.

2nd row: Needle cases; silver, sterling and plate; $40.00 – 75.00.
1., 2. England; sterling, marked "SP" (Samuel Pemberton); c. 1790, $65.00.
3. England, marked "Birmingham, sterling, 1890" (also a darner); $75.00.
4., 5. China, coin silver; c. 1890, $65.00 – 75.00.
6. Mexico; maker's mark, peanut reproduction, made for export during Jimmy Carter's term as president, 1976 – 1980; $3.00 – 5.00.
7., 9. USA, silver, sterling; c. 1900, 1920, $45.00 – 60.00.
8. Mexico, Taxco; marker's mark; "900"; c. 1910, $25.00.

3rd row: Needle cases; vegetable ivory/bone.
1. – 4. England; cases with metal fittings (brass); c. 1875, $20.00 – 30.00.
5. – 7. Asia; bone; c. 1890, $20.00 – 35.00.
8. USA; Northwest Native American figure; (tusk) 2¾"; c. 1900, $95.00.
9., 10., 13. – 15.; Asia; bone; c. 1880, $20.00 – 65.00.
11. France; mother-of-pearl; 4½"; finial missing; c. 1875, $45.00.
12. France; paper label "made in France, silk loop with amber bead; vegetable ivory; c. 1875, $125.00.

1st row: Nanny pins; gold fill of two colors, goldstone mounting, one end of cylinder in bar unscrews and is a holder for a needle and thread, also called nanny brooch; c. 1875, $150.00 – 275.00.

1. Marked "DRCM2680036," goldstone set on point, beveled edge-finish; 1⅞".
2. Marked "Gesdesch," round goldstone; 2⅞".

2nd row:

1. England; star shape, cut glass settings, gold fill; c. 1880, $125.00.

3rd row:

1. England; nanny pin and its removable needle cylinder for thread and needle; 2⅓"; c. 1875, $150.00 – 275.00.

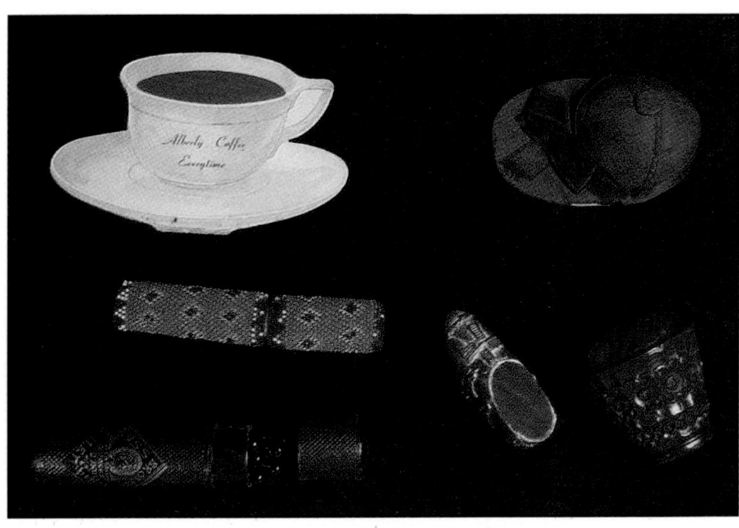

1st row:

1. USA; needle holder; cup and saucer; paper die cut, coffee ad; c. 1915, $55.00.
2. England; pincushion jockey-style hat; silk covered; c. 1900, $50.00.

2nd row:

1. England; needle holder; bone cyclinder covered with glass beadwork; c. 1890, $130.00.
2. Shoe; Dutch-style with embossed men and women, velvet cushion, pot metal; c. 1900, $25.00.
3. Asia; pincushion; vegetable ivory, filigree carving; c. 1880, $50.00.
4. Germany; holder; glass head pins, painted wood; c. 1900, $20.00.

1st row:
1. USA; Caribbean-style headdress; felt; face pieces glued on; felt for needles; c. 1915, $15.00.
2. England; folder; illustrated cover; c. 1900, $35.00.
3. Asia; book; pierced ivory blue silk lining; 1" x 2"; c. 1875, $90.00.
4. England; needle kit; leather with gold lettering, Milward's Helix Needles, 5 packets; c. 1890, $20.00.

2nd row: USA holders
1. Sweet Grass, wool pages; c. 1920, $30.00.
2. Suede folder, decorative cross stitch, wool pages; c. 1920, $10.00.
3. Butterfly; painted velvet, wire and beading embellishments; c. 1900, $25.00.

3rd row: USA holders
1. Polished metal, snap top; c. 1920, $30.00.
2. Brass with velvet lining, spring closure; c. 1930, $20.00.
3. Boye Co., slide closure, #8 sharps, "Patent July 23, 1912." $40.00.

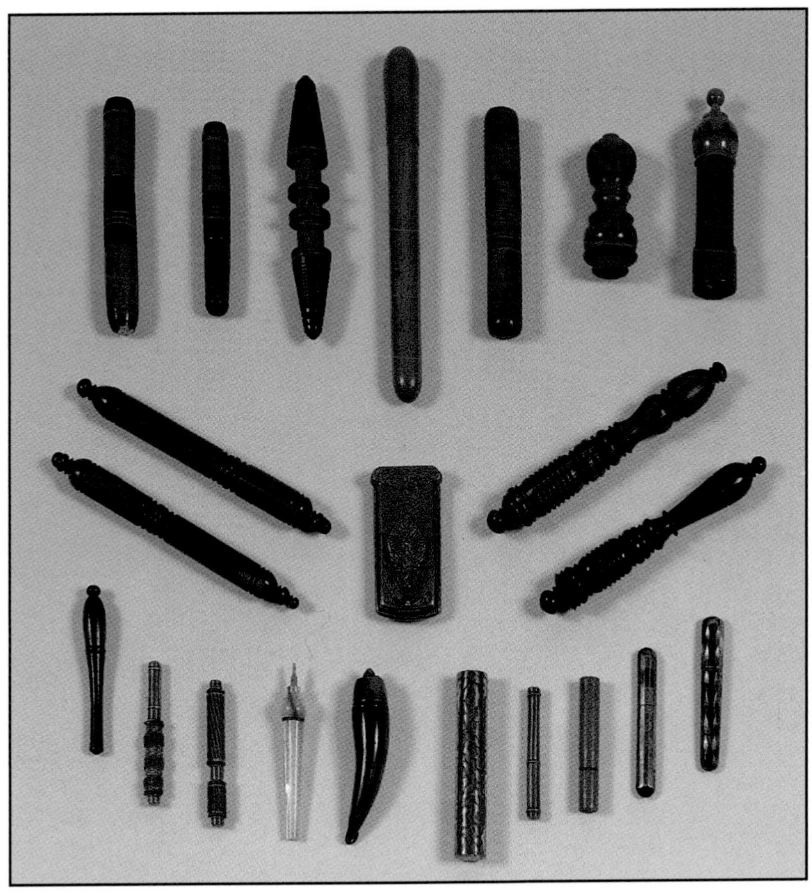

Top row: Needle cases

1., 2., 5. England; wood, painted; c. 1880, $30.00 each.
3. Italy; two different woods, intricate carving and overlay; 4½"; c. 1875, $65.00.
4. England; maple, contains a number of different sizes of needles; 6½"; c. 1900, $35.00.
6. Asia; Vegetable ivory, hand carved; 2½"; c. 1880, $45.00.
7. Bulgarian; column; painted, varnished wood, souvenir; 3¾"; 1985, $15.00.

2nd row: Needle cases

1., 2., 4., 5. England; wood, 3 yew, 1 ebony; reproduction of traditional designs; maker Guy Ravine, Weedom; hand turned; 1994, $45.00 each.
3. England; "Quadruple Golden Casket" for packets of size 6 and 7 needles, W. Avery & Son, Redditch; 2¾"; c. 1870, $90.00.

3rd row: Needle cases

1., 8. England; wood, #8 natural finish, #1 marbleized paint and varnish; c. 1890, $30.00 – 45.00.
2., 3. England; brass cylinder with braided decorative wire; c. 1870, $40.00 – 50.00.
4. France; mother-of-pearl with gold fill fitting; c. 1875, $60.00.
5. USA; Northern Plains; horn; wire ring in tip; 3"; c. 1900, $25.00.
6. Germany; celluloid with silver overlay design, 3⅜"; c. 1920, $25.00.
7. England; brass; c. 1875, $25.00.
9., 10. England; cut steel beveled and diamond design; c. 1820, $40.00.

1st row: Needle holders

1. – 5. Germany; wood made for export, angled arrow trademark, turn top for ejecting needles, multiple sizes; c. 1880, $60.00 – 75.00.
6. Asia; column with crown top, hand-carved vegetable ivory; c. 1880, $60.00.

2nd row:

1. England; matchbox shape, painted, varnished paper with gold lettering, "J. J. Michi 4 Leadenhall St, London"; c. 1910, $40.00.
2. France; lady; carved, painted (originally paired with a man); c. 1875, $75.00.
3. England; ebony, varnished decal "Marine Parade Boconor"; 3¼"; c. 1900, $25.00.
4. South America; corozo seed from a palm tree, has hardness and carving qualities that allow for close, repetitive designs, takes on a honey color when exposed to light. NPA.

3rd row:

1. USA; needle stand; ebony and sterling, needles #1 – 9 and needle threader; marked "Patent Feb. 22, 1916 made in USA, Tube 0, Style d6"; $150.00.
2. USA; butterfly needle threader; painted wood; $25.00.
3. England; cylinder, painted over brass, "A. Farr & Sons, Redditch," size #4 – 8 needles, screwtop; 2¼"; c. 1880, $20.00.

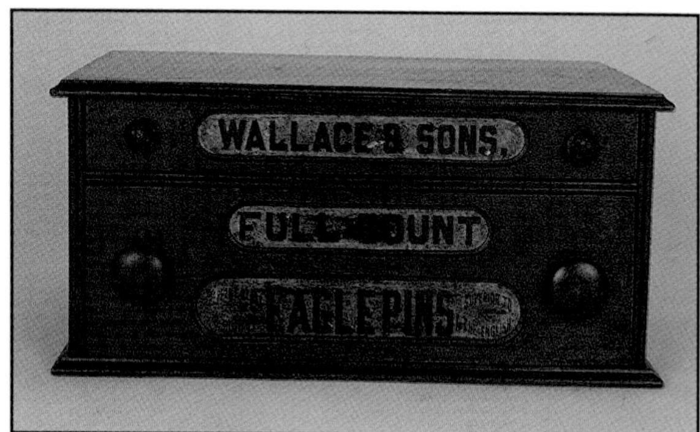

USA; Wallace Sons Full Count Eagle pins; all original store counter display and storage chest; $450.00.

Advertisements: Paper

1st row:

1. Clover, made in Czechoslovakia, trademark-turtle, "Yours for snaps," $20.00.
2. Rhineland, Germany; "Piccadilly"; 1 packet large eye sharps, $4.00.
3. USA; Pensacola, Florida; Hannah Pharmacy; 1 packet, $3.00.
4. USA; Equitable Life Insurance Co.; Dix Rands, high grade needle; 1935. $7.50.

2nd row:

1. USA; Worcester Iodized Salt; die cut, USA patent; German, "Queen Victoria," silver-eye sharps; c. 1915, $25.00.
2. England; Holbrook Worcestershire Sauce; die cut, #8 sharps; inside: "Needles and Pins, produced in England." "What sauce is good for the goose, we are told, is sauce for the gander, too." "That Holbrook's sauce is the sauce for the world. Is a saying equally true." c. 1915, $30.00.
3. Japan; Army/Navy needle book; superior drill eyed sharps, 4 packets; c. 1920, $7.50.
4. England; toilet pins; Abel Morrell's, Cross/Fox trademark; c. 1900, $7.50.
5. USA; Stewart's silk pins; brass, rust proof, ½ box; c. 1940, $7.50.

3rd row: #1–9 $1.00 – 10.00.

1. England; Hempstead; G. W. MEYER, General Draper; #7 sharps "25 egg eyes for one penny"; c. 1900.
2. England; Queen's Crewel; T. Harper Manufacturer, Redditch.
3. England; Redditch; Flora MacDonald; Morell's Cross/Fox trademark; #4/8" betweens; c. 1910.
4. Occupied Japan; standard high grade, Dix Rands "Queen Victoria" #3/9 sharps.
5. England; Schul Sons sharps; US Patent Office Seal 1877.
6. England; Redditch; H. Milward and Sons; betweens.
7. Czechoslovakia; Superior (SKS) #1/6 sharps.
8. Germany; Dix Rands #3/9 sharps.
9. USA; Kentucky; Lexington Ice Co.; c. 1920.

4th row:

1. England; "Florence"; brass turn top, painted wood, "John Thompson & Co., New York, sole agent for James Smith & Sons"; c. 1900, $15.00.
2. England; Crowley's; Lion Brand Crewel Embroidery #5 needles.
3. England; Milward's needles; "War Pack," #5/10 embroidery; c. 1915.
4. Redditch, England; yarn darners; Brabant Needle Co. #14/18 needles.
5. England; "KABECOM," "War Pack," #3/9 sharps; c. 1915.
6. England; Redditch; coat of arms #7 sharps.
7. England; Universal nickel plated #4/8 sharps.
8. England; sailmaker's needles; W. Smith & Son, "Needles in this pack are made expressly to meet the requirements of American Sailmakers"; c. 1890. #2. – 8. $15.00.

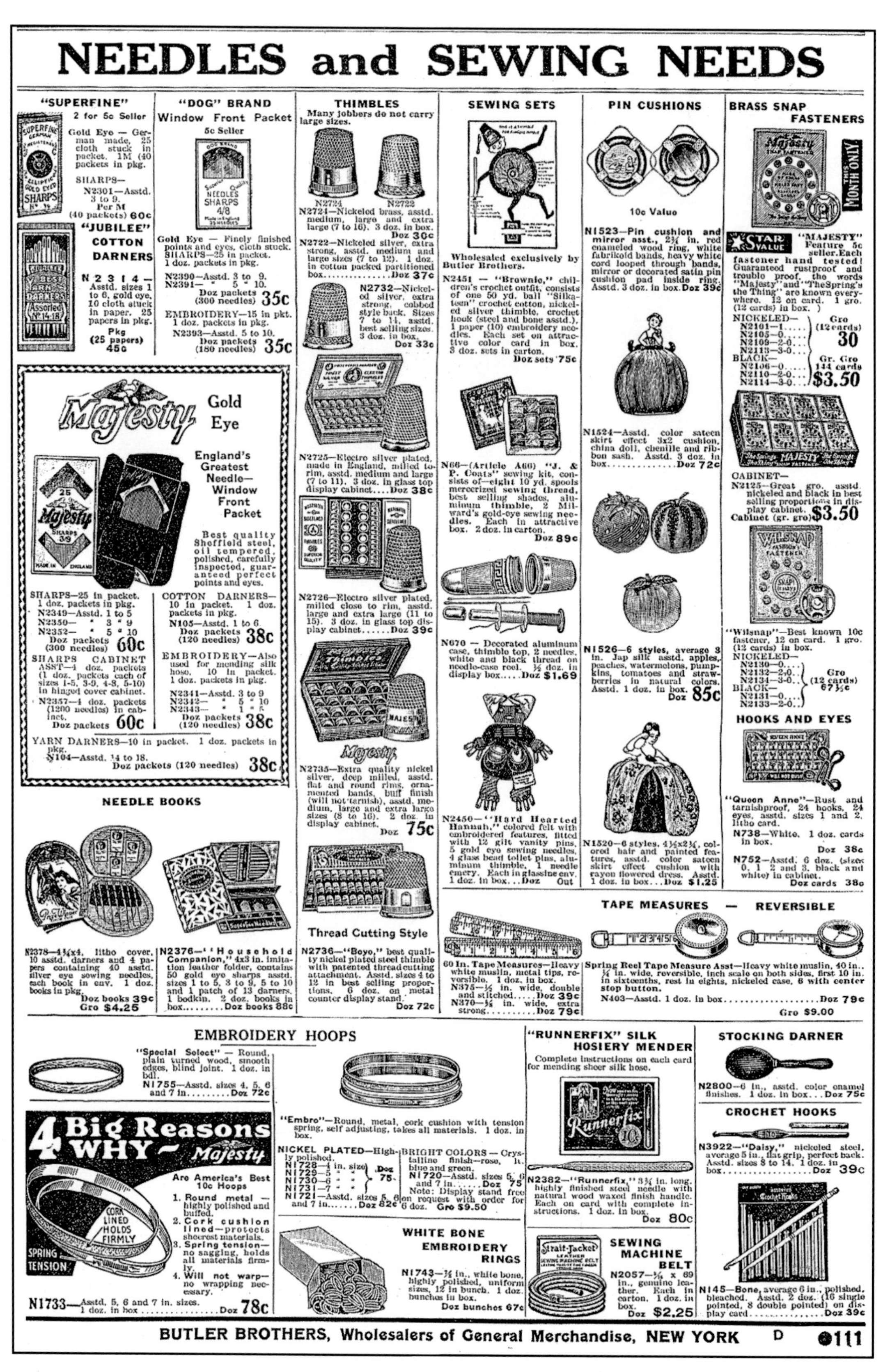

NEEDLES and SEWING NEEDS

"SUPERFINE"
2 for 5c Seller
Gold Eye — German made, 25 cloth stuck in packet. 1M (40 packets in pkg.
SHARPS—
N2301—Asstd. 3 to 9. Per M (40 packets) 60c

"JUBILEE" COTTON DARNERS
N2314—Asstd. sizes 1 to 6, gold eye, 10 cloth stuck in paper. 25 papers in pkg. Pkg (25 papers) 45c

"DOG" BRAND
Window Front Packet
5c Seller
Gold Eye — Finely finished points and eyes, cloth stuck. SHARPS—25 in packet. 1 doz. packets in pkg.
N2390—Asstd. 3 to 9.
N2391— " 5 " 10.
Doz packets (300 needles) 35c
EMBROIDERY—15 in pkt. 1 doz. packets in pkg.
N2393—Asstd. 5 to 10. Doz packets (180 needles) 35c

Majesty Gold Eye
England's Greatest Needle—Window Front Packet
Best quality Sheffield steel, oil tempered, polished, carefully inspected, guaranteed perfect points and eyes.
SHARPS—25 in packet. 1 doz. packets in pkg.
N2349—Asstd. 1 to 5
N2350— " 3 " 9
N2352— " 5 " 10
Doz packets (300 needles) 60c
SHARPS CABINET ASST—4 doz. packets (1 doz. packets each of sizes 1-5, 3-9, 4-8, 5-10) in hinged cover cabinet.
N2357—4 doz. packets (1200 needles) in cabinet. Doz packets 60c
COTTON DARNERS—10 in packet. 1 doz. packets in pkg.
N105—Asstd. 1 to 6. Doz packets (120 needles) 38c
EMBROIDERY—Also used for mending silk hose. 10 in packet. 1 doz. packets in pkg.
N2341—Asstd. 3 to 9
N2342— " 5 " 10
N2343— " 1 " 5
Doz packets (120 needles) 38c
YARN DARNERS—10 in packet. 1 doz. packets in pkg.
N104—Asstd. 14 to 18. Doz packets (120 needles) 38c

NEEDLE BOOKS
N2378—4¾x4, litho cover, 10 asstd. darners and 4 papers containing 40 asstd. silver eye sewing needles, each book in env. 1 doz. books in pkg. Doz books 39c Gro $4.25
N2376—"Household Companion," 4x3 in. imitation leather folder, contains 50 gold eye sharps asstd. sizes 1 to 5, 3 to 9, 5 to 10 and 1 patch of 13 darners, 1 bodkin. 2 doz. books in box.........Doz books 88c

THIMBLES
Many jobbers do not carry large sizes.
N2724 N2722
N2724—Nickeled brass, asstd. medium, large and extra large (7 to 16). 3 doz. in box. Doz 30c
N2722—Nickeled silver, extra strong, asstd. medium and large sizes (7 to 12). 1 doz. in cotton packed partitioned box..............Doz 37c
N2732—Nickeled silver, extra strong, cobbed style back. Sizes 7 to 14, asstd. best selling sizes. 3 doz. in box. Doz 33c
N2725—Electro silver plated, made in England, milled to rim, asstd. medium and large (7 to 11). 3 doz. in glass top display cabinet....Doz 38c
N2726—Electro silver plated, milled close to rim, asstd. large and extra large (11 to 15). 3 doz. in glass top display cabinet......Doz 39c
Majesty
N2735—Extra quality nickel silver, deep milled, asstd. flat and round rims, ornamented bands, buff finish (will not tarnish), asstd. medium, large and extra large sizes (8 to 16). 2 doz. in display cabinet. Doz 75c
Thread Cutting Style
N2736—"Boyo," best quality nickel plated steel thimble with patented thread cutting attachment. Asstd. sizes 4 to 12 in best selling proportions. 6 doz. on metal counter display stand. Doz 72c

SEWING SETS
Wholesaled exclusively by Butler Brothers.
N2451 — "Brownie," children's crochet outfit, consists of one 50 yd. ball "Silkateen" crochet cotton, nickeled silver thimble, crochet hook (steel and bone asstd.), 1 paper (10) embroidery needles. Each set on attractive color card in box. 3 doz. sets in carton. Doz sets 75c
N66—(Article A66) "J. & P. Coats" sewing kit, consists of—eight 10 yd. spools mercerized sewing thread, best selling shades, aluminum thimble, 2 Milward's gold-eye sewing needles. Each in attractive box. 2 doz. in carton. Doz 89c
N670 — Decorated aluminum case, thimble top, 2 needles, white and black thread on needle-case reel. ½ doz. in display box.....Doz $1.69
N2450—"Hard Hearted Hannah," colored felt with embroidered features, fitted with 12 gilt vanity pins, 5 gold eye sewing needles, 4 glass bead toilet pins, aluminum thimble, 1 needle emery. Each in glassine env. 1 doz. in box...Doz Out

PIN CUSHIONS
10c Value
N1523—Pin cushion and mirror asst., 2¾ in. red enameled wood ring, white fabrikoid bands, heavy white cord looped through bands, mirror or decorated satin pin cushion pad inside ring. Asstd. 3 doz. in box. Doz 39c
N1524—Asstd. color sateen skirt effect 3x2 cushion, china doll, chenille and ribbon sash. Asstd. 3 doz. in box..............Doz 72c
N1526—6 styles, average 3 in. Jap silk asstd. apples, peaches, watermelons, pumpkins, tomatoes and strawberries in natural colors. Asstd. 1 doz. in box. Doz 85c
N1520—6 styles, 4½x2¾, colored hair and painted features, asstd. color sateen skirt effect cushion with rayon flowered dress. Asstd. 1 doz. in box...Doz $1.25

BRASS SNAP FASTENERS
THIS MONTH ONLY
STAR VALUE "MAJESTY" Feature 5c seller. Each fastener hand tested! Guaranteed rustproof and trouble proof, the words "Majesty" and "The Spring's the Thing" are known everywhere. 12 on card. 1 gro. (12 cards) in box.
NICKELED—
N2101—1.....
N2105—0.....
N2109—2-0...
N2113—3-0...
Gro (12 cards) 30
BLACK—
N2106—0.....
N2110—2-0...
N2114—3-0...
Gr. Gro 144 cards $3.50
CABINET—
N2125—Great gro. asstd. nickeled and black in best selling proportions in display cabinet. Cabinet (gr. gro) $3.50
"Wilsnap"—Best known 10c fastener, 12 on card. 1 gro. (12 cards) in box.
NICKELED—
N2130—0....
N2132—2-0..
N2134—3-0..
BLACK—
N2131—0....
N2133—2-0..
Gro (12 cards) 67½c

HOOKS AND EYES
"Queen Anne"—Rust and tarnishproof, 24 hooks, 24 eyes, asstd. sizes 1 and 2, litho card.
N738—White. 1 doz. cards in box. Doz 38c
N752—Asstd. 6 doz. (sizes 0, 1 2 and 3, black and white) in cabinet. Doz cards 38c

TAPE MEASURES — REVERSIBLE
60 In. Tape Measures—Heavy white muslin, metal tips, reversible. 1 doz. in box.
N375—½ in. wide, double and stitched.....Doz 39c
N370—⅝ in. wide, extra strong..........Doz 79c
Spring Reel Tape Measure Asst—Heavy white muslin, 40 in., ¼ in. wide, reversible, inch scale on both sides, first 10 in. in sixteenths, rest in eights, nickeled case, 6 with center stop button.
N403—Asstd. 1 doz. in box....................Doz 79c Gro $9.00

EMBROIDERY HOOPS
"Special Select" — Round, plain turned wood, smooth edges, blind joint. 1 doz. in bdl.
N1755—Asstd. sizes 4, 5, 6 and 7 in.........Doz 72c
4 Big Reasons WHY — Majesty
Are America's Best 10c Hoops
1. Round metal — highly polished and buffed.
2. Cork cushion lined—protects sheerest materials.
3. Spring tension—no sagging, holds all materials firmly.
4. Will not warp—no wrapping necessary.
CORK LINED HOLDS FIRMLY
SPRING TENSION
N1733—Asstd. 5, 6 and 7 in. sizes. 1 doz. in box ....Doz 78c
"Embro"—Round, metal, cork cushion with tension spring, self adjusting, takes all materials. 1 doz. in box.
NICKEL PLATED—Highly polished.
N1728—4 in. size
N1729—5 " "
N1730—6 " "
N1731—7 " "
Doz 75
N1721—Asstd. sizes 5, 6 and 7 in.......Doz 82c
BRIGHT COLORS — Crystalline finish—rose, lt. blue and green.
N1720—Asstd. sizes 5, 6 and 7 in.......Doz 75
Note: Display stand free on request with order for 6 doz. Gro $9.50

WHITE BONE EMBROIDERY RINGS
N1743—¾ in., white bone, highly polished, uniform sizes, 12 in bunch. 1 doz. bunches in box. Doz bunches 67c

"RUNNERFIX" SILK HOSIERY MENDER
Complete instructions on each card for mending sheer silk hose.
N2382—"Runnerfix," 3¾ in. long, highly finished steel needle with natural wood waxed finish handle. Each on card with complete instructions. 1 doz. in box. Doz 80c

SEWING MACHINE BELT
N2057—¼ x 69 in., genuine leather. Each in carton. 1 doz. in box. Doz $2.25

STOCKING DARNER
N2800—6 in., asstd. color enamel finishes. 1 doz. in box...Doz 75c

CROCHET HOOKS
N3922—"Daisy," nickeled steel, average 5 in., flat grip, perfect back. Asstd. sizes 8 to 14. 1 doz. in box..................Doz 39c
N145—Bone, average 6 in., polished, bleached. Asstd. 2 doz. (16 single pointed, 8 double pointed) on display card................Doz 39c

BUTLER BROTHERS, Wholesalers of General Merchandise, NEW YORK D 111

Butler Brothers ad, January, 1929.

Chapter Two

Thimbles

There has been very little change in the design of the thimble since its discovery in the volcanic rubble of Mount Vesuvius, in the Roman ruins of England, and in other excavation sites around the world. The earliest example found is an open-ended thimble dating from 79 AD. The dome, or flat top thimble, dates from the thirteenth century and is marked with handmade indentations. The thimbles with messages and mottoes, as well as the very elegant thimbles, evolved in the sixteenth century. At the same time, steel thimbles, as well as needles, came into Europe from the steel manufacturers of the East. Porcelain thimbles were introduced in the nineteenth century, and Miessen of Saxony dominated this production by 1875. Miessen was the only porcelain manufacturer to use Chinese designs. Although the porcelain thimble was considered more decorative than useful, there were some who felt the smooth surface preferable when working with silk. Thimbles have been made of every conceivable material that would protect the finger or hand when sewing. Some have been made just for collecting (see pages 43 – 49) and were used to commemorate historic events, individuals, and other subjects of interest.

Holders for thimbles range from simple containers to more imaginative and elegant displays. The holders aided in retarding rust and/or tarnish, and they provided a safe storage place. For collectors, it is very rare to find the original thimble and its holder together. Thimbles have been a favorite item for collector for many years. Note the terms "solid silver" and "solid gold" and the lack of a manufacturer name credit in the Sears advertisements on pages 37 and 39.

1st row:

1. Dutch; brass, hand punched; c. 1600s, $25.00.
2. England; two fused together, machine punched; c. 1700s, $35.00.
3. England; brass, machine punched; c. 1700s, $35.00.

2nd row:

1. England; bronze, hand punched, tailor's thimble; c. 1300s, $45.00.
2. England; cast bronze, hand punched, tailor's thimble; c. 1400s, $45.00.
3. England; brass, hand punched, out of Thames River excavation; c. 1500, $35.00.

France; the two or more colors of gold used on thimbles were fashionable during the eighteenth century and early nineteenth century. One color was used for the decorative bands and the other for the body of the thimble; c. 1780. $1,800.00.

1st row:

1. – 3., 7. Simons Bros. Company, 14 carat; $135.00.
4. Simons Bros. Company, engraved "K," framed band with seed pearl in each frame; $140.00.
5. Simons Bros. Company, engraved "AMW" '08"; $135.00.
6. Simons Bros. Company, engraved "P"; $120.00.
8. Simons mark, "full carat weight mark"; $140.00.

2nd row:

1. – 11. No maker's mark, 14 carat; c. 1910, $120.00 – $200.00.
   1. Engraved "Abbie 1870."

3rd row:

1. – 8. 10 carat; c. 1920. $100.00.
   1. Simons Bros. Company, scalloped edge.
   2. No mark, village scene.
3. – 5. Stern Bros Co.
   3. Engraved "H-L-B 6-22-20."
6. – 8. No maker's mark.

1st row:

1., 2. H. Muhr's Sons, 14 carat; $120.00.
3., 4. Simons Bros. Company, 14 carat; $120.00.
5. Carter, Gough & Co, 14 carat; $120.00.
6. No maker's mark, marked 18 carat inside band; $240.00.
7., 8. Stern Brothers & Co, gold fill; $60.00.
9. Schorndorf, Germany; Gabler Bros., 14 carat, damascene style band; $110.00.

2nd row: Sterling with gold bands; $65.00 – 75.00.

1. – 7., 12., 13. Simons Bros. Company.
8. No maker's mark.
9., 10. Ketcham & McDougal.
11. Stern Bros.

1st row:

1. – 5., 7. – 9. Ketcham & McDougal, sterling; $35.00 – 65.00.
6. Louis IV band; $70.00.

2nd row:

1. – 15. Simons Bros. Company, sterling; $30.00 – 60.00.
1. A raised design of vines and grapes; $85.00.
4. A 3-D design of garlands and cherubs; $150.00.

3rd row:

England; silver; $40.00 – 75.00.

1. Birmingham, 1904.
2. Birmingham, stamped "Royal Spa," 1911.
3. Dorcas.
4. Birmingham, 1902.
5. Dorcas.
6. Birmingham, "James Walker wishes you luck," ad, 1924.
7. Chester, 1918.
8. New Castle, 1881.
9. Scandinavia, dark red stone cap.
10. Birmingham, 1926.
11. Chester, 1920.

1st row: 1.–8. Tailor's thimbles; no maker's mark; $10.00 – 35.00.

1. England; nickel over brass.
2. Germany; polished metal, brass rolled edge.
3. USA; polished metal.
4. USA; sterling.
5. Marked "825," decorative band.
6. England; marked "Birmingham, sterling, 1891."
7. Coin silver.
8. USA; sterling.

2nd row: 1.– 6. No maker's mark.

1. India; ivory; c. 1850, $50.00.
2. China; ivory, made for export as part of a sewing box; c. 1860, $60.00.
3. Vegetable ivory; c. 1875, $75.00.
4. China; pierced jade; c. 1875, $85.00.
5., 6. China; cloisonné; 1980, 1992, $15.00.
7., 8. Simons Brothers Co.; industrial alloy, band leaf design; $15.00.
9. Germany; Gabler Bros., "800" silver, floral swag design on band; $35.00.
10. Austria; nickel, floral band; $12.00.

3rd row:

1., 2. USA; sterling, no maker's mark, band pastoral scene; $35.00.
3. USA; Waite, Thresher Co., sterling; $30.00.
4. USA; Towle, "925" silver. $35.00.
5. England; no maker's mark, size 3, palm fron band design; $32.00.
6. USA; no maker's mark, sterling; $25.00.
7. USA; no maker's mark, sterling, miniature or game piece; ½"; $60.00.
8. USA; no maker's mark, sterling; $20.00.
9., 10. USA; pot metal, game thimble or prize, "for a good girl" on band; ½", ¾"; $5.00 – 10.00.
11. USA; painted china, "Fairy Thimble"; $10.00.

Sears Roebuck & Co., 1927.

1st row:
- 1.– 4. Sterling, no maker's mark; $30.00 – 40.00.
- 5. Sterling, no maker's mark, "Pat. Sep. 20, '01"; $65.00.
- 6.– 9. Stern Brothers Co., sterling; $30.00 – 45.00.
- 10., 11. Webster Company, sterling, raised flower design; $45.00.

2nd row:
- 1.– 9. Simons Brothers Co., sterling; $35.00 – 45.00.
- 10.– 13. Waite, Thresher & Co, sterling; $30.00 – 55.00.

3rd row:
- 1.– 4., 6.– 8. Wait, Thresher & Co., sterling; $30.00 – 50.00.
- 2. Engraved "Helen."
- 3., 8. Raised flower designs.
- 5. Decorative geometric band, $30.00.
- 9. H. Muhr's Sons, sterling; c. 1900, $30.00.
- 10. Germany; sterling, "925," band of raised leaves, amber glass top; $75.00.

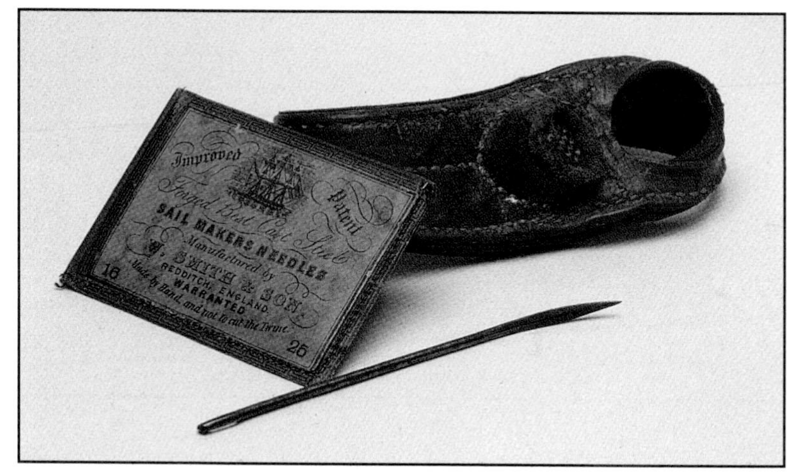

1st row:
1. Sailmaker's thimble/sailor's palm; leather with a heavy brass disc, machine punched indentations for pushing the needle when sewing; c. 1900, $50.00.
2., 3. Sailmakers' needle packet and single needle. (See Chapter 1, page 31.)

1st row:

1. USA; pierced sterling thimble holder, Webster Co.; c. 1875, $110.00.
2. USA; sterling, decorative band with cats playing with a ball; c. 1975 (reproduction), $45.00.
3. Germany; silver marked "925" and "M"; Gabler Bros., enameled band with decorative tulips; c. 1915, $95.00.
4. Russia; silver, marked "900"; niello style; souvenir; c. 1980, $35.00.
5. USA; sterling; possibly a child's thimble; size 4; c. 1920, $30.00.
6. USA; sterling; doll thimble; originally paired with a child's thimble that was the same design made for a girl; ⅜"; c. 1915, $60.00.

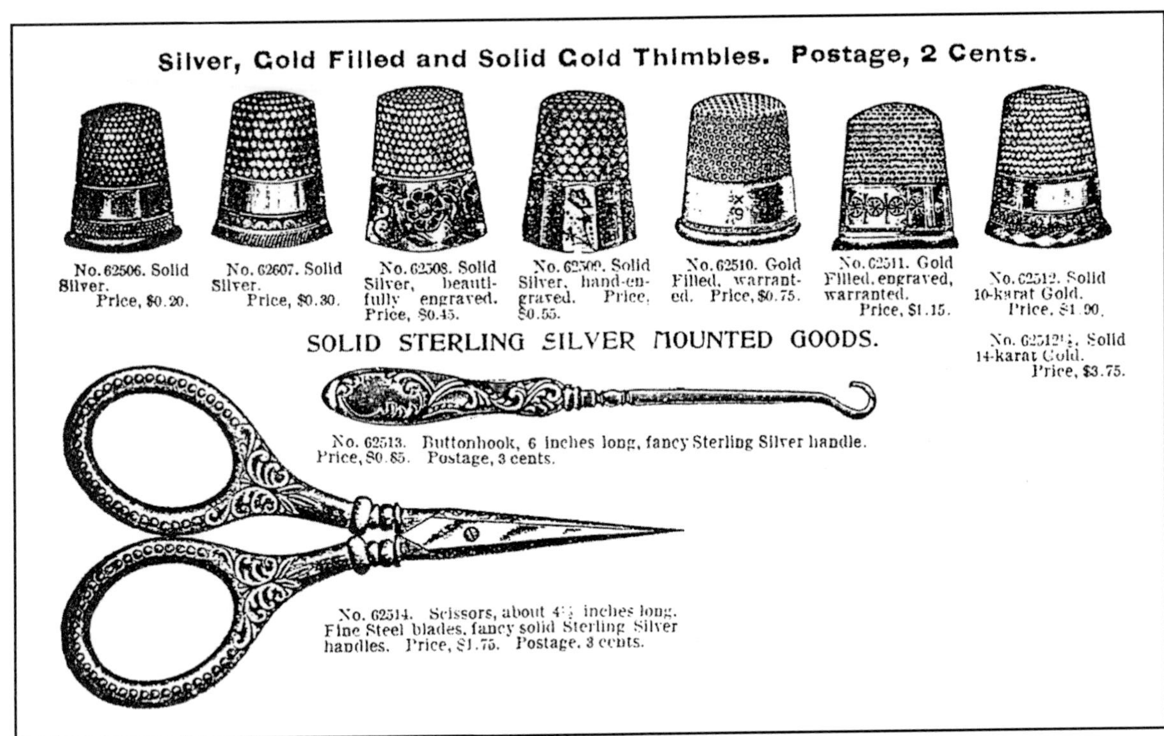

Silver, Gold Filled and Solid Gold Thimbles. Postage, 2 Cents.

No. 62506. Solid Silver. Price, $0.20.

No. 62607. Solid Silver. Price, $0.30.

No. 62508. Solid Silver, beautifully engraved. Price, $0.45.

No. 62509. Solid Silver, hand-engraved. Price, $0.55.

No. 62510. Gold Filled, warranted. Price, $0.75.

No. 62511. Gold Filled, engraved, warranted. Price, $1.15.

No. 62512. Solid 10-karat Gold. Price, $1.90.

No. 62512½. Solid 14-karat Gold. Price, $3.75.

SOLID STERLING SILVER MOUNTED GOODS.

No. 62513. Buttonhook, 6 inches long, fancy Sterling Silver handle. Price, $0.85. Postage, 3 cents.

No. 62514. Scissors, about 4½ inches long. Fine Steel blades, fancy solid Sterling Silver handles. Price, $1.75. Postage, 3 cents.

Sears catalog, 1897.

1st row:

1. USA; Simons Brothers Company, sterling, Liberty Bell band "Proclaim in the land to the inhabitants. By the order of the Assembly of Philadelphia 1752"; c. 1915, $100.00.
2. Holland; enamel on metal, flower spray, "Bicentennial 1976," Betsy Ross & US flag; 1976, $45.00.
3. England; marked Birmingham, sterling, Queen's mark, "Silver Jubilee Of ER II"; 1977, $100.00.
4. USA; Kentucky, "KHQS" (Kentucky Heritage Quilt Society), glazed pottery, limited edition; 1982, NPA.
5. USA; Paducah, Kentucky, American Quilter's Society; Simons Brothers Company, sterling, limited edition; 1986, $80.00.
6. USA; Simons Brothers Company, sterling, National Quilting Assoc.; on band: "Charleston, WV, NQA, Silver Jubilee 1994," limited edition; $65.00.
7. China; glazed bone china with transfer "THE NAMES PROJECT"; $15.00.

2nd row:

1. Mexico; sterling; $10.00.
2. USA; Navajo, sterling with spider turquoise set; 1994, $25.00.
3. Mexico; abalone and mother of pearl inlay over silver; c. 1980, $20.00.
4. USA; Navajo, Herbert Begay, signed and stamped, 14 carat gold with spider turquoise set; $450.00.

5., 7. Scandinavia; coin silver; $40.00.

6., 8. Mexico; coin silver; $20.00.

3rd row: 1.–6., 8. England, brass.

1. "Use Hudson Soap"; $35.00.
2. Plain; $10.00.
3. "Her Majesty Thimble," company name; $25.00.
4. Fan design; c. 1890, $25.00.
5. "Made in England," "Piccadilly, New York"; $30.00.
6. "Love you"; $20.00.
7. Copper, heart design on band; $20.00.
8. Leaf design on band; $12.00.
9. Nickel over brass; $10.00.
10. Copper, collector's thimble, "Are you a Digitabulus?"; $35.00.

1st row:

1. Austria; fine china, Hansel and Gretel; 1989.
2. Austria; fine china, Christmas; 1990.
3. Austria; fine china, Valentine; 1990.
4., 6.– 8. Glass with paperweight-style design in glass top.
5. Glass, etched design of flowers.

2nd row:

1. Filigree, 10 carat gold, blue floral enamel; $75.00.
2. England; sterling, with 10 carat band and coral; $85.00.
3. USA, Leadville, Colorado; brass (recycled cartridge shell), turquoise top, "RB 1984"; $35.00.
4. Sterling, with coral in band design; $80.00
5. England; sterling, agate top; $75.00.
6. Germany; Gabler Bros, sterling, diamond shape sets with coral on band; $75.00.
7. France; copper with thin blue enameled band; $30.00.
8. Germany; copper with blue stone top; c. 1920, $50.00.

3rd row: Enamel over sterling

1. USA; Simons Brothers Company, floral band; $60.00.
2. England, Birmingham; blue point Siamese cat transfer; $40.00.
3. England, Birmingham; two Oriental scenes with birds; $60.00.
4. Norway; blue-ribbed; $75.00.
5. Norway; reindeer-drawn sled, moonstone cap; $125.00.
6. Norway; roses; $90.00.
7. Germany; Gabler Bros., Dutch scene; $90.00.
8. West Germany; bluebird; $45.00.
9. Germany; Gabler Bros., roses, pink stone top; $95.00.
10. France; "830 silver," roses, dark blue stone top; $150.00.
11. Germany; swag of roses, green stone top; $75.00.
12. Germany; rose band, red stone top; $100.00.
13. Germany; Gabler Bros., "925," roses; $70.00
14. West Germany; Gabler Bros., French scene transfer; $40.00.

1st row:

1. USA; Holiday Musicians' Train, pewter, musicians on flat cars. NPA.

2nd row: #1 – 10: $10.00 – 50.00.

1. USA; Louisville, Kentucky; Louisville Stoneware pottery.
2. USA; elk horn capped with buffalo horn, buffalo transfer.
3., 4. USA, Alaska; whale tooth, handmade.
5. Africa; ox horn.
6. USA, West Virginia; coal.
7. Heatherwood, stag antler cap.
8. Oxen horn.
9. Snake skin covering.
10. USA, Alaska; seal skin thimble, gut thread, bone needle.

3rd row: #1 – 12: USA, $3.00 – 6.00.

1. Plastic; Re-elect d'Alesandro for Mayor '86.
2. Plastic; National Quilting Assoc., Silver Jubilee, 1994, $10.00.
3. Aluminum; White Sewing Machine.
4. – 7. Singer Sewing Machine, $4.00.
8. Plastic, "PTPFTWTTYP."
9. Albany, NY; plastic, electrical appliances.
10. Decatur, Ill.; plastic, First Federal.
11. "Serve the Lord with gladness," Ps. 100:2.
12. Plastic, plain.

Avon Ladies made in Taiwan, ROC; hand-painted porcelain. The date of the fashions represented is as follows: 1927, 1947, 1900, 1923, 1942, 1938, 1928, 1890. NPA.

Country Store thimbles have copies of original label designs of household items. They were issued by The Franklin Mint, Franklin Center, PA. There is 24 carat gold trim near the top and rim and they are porcelain. 1980. NPA.

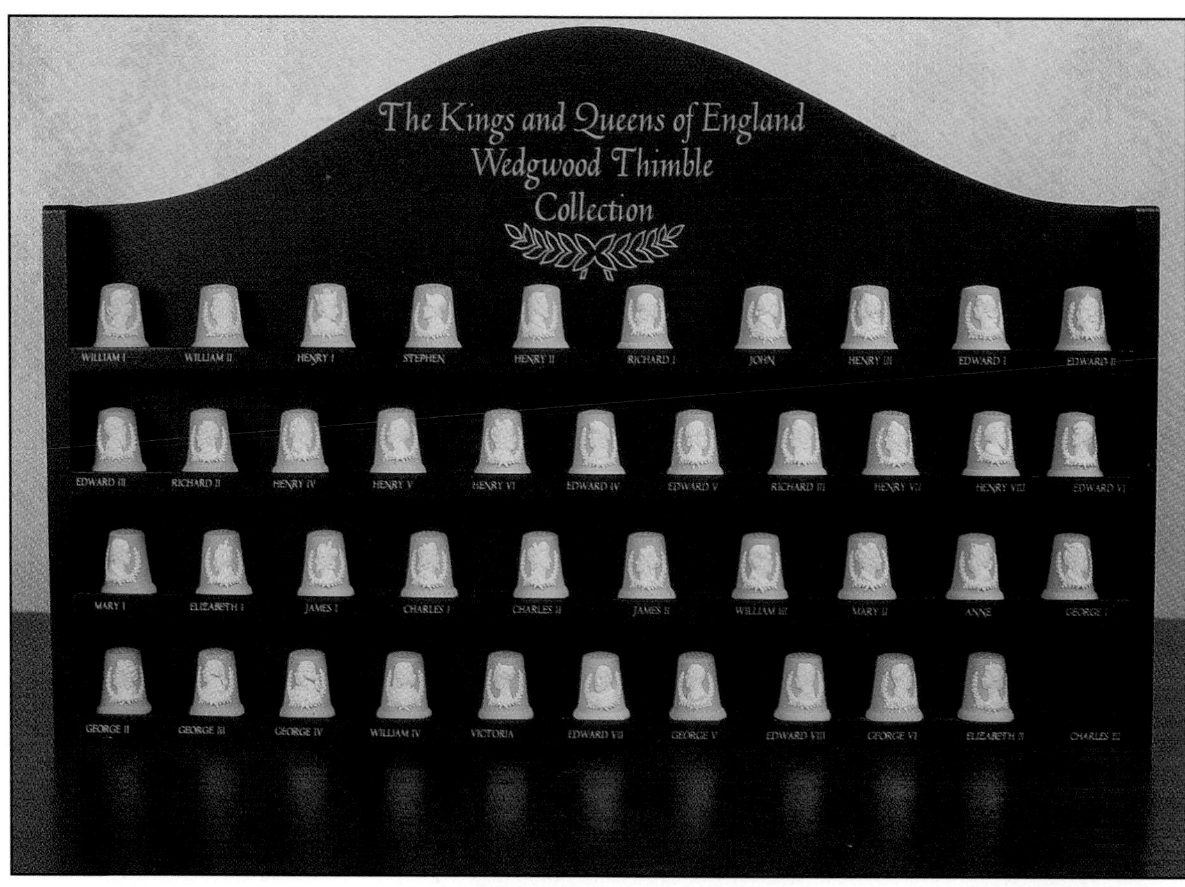

The Kings and Queens of England were issued on the 250th anniversary of Josiah Wedgwood's birthday. He was the "Father of English potters." This was a limited edition of 20,000 issued by Calhoun's Collectors Society, Inc., Minneapolis, MN.

Josiah Wedgwood was from Barlaston, Stoke-on-Trent, England. The Wedgwood factory has documentation that it has been producing jasperware items since the mid-eighteenth century. Thimbles were among those items.

This collection is the first to be issued by Wedgwood, first jasper thimble collection bearing cameo portraits, first Wedgwood collection of miniature cameo portraits, and first Wedgwood collection of any kind bearing cameos of all 41 monarchs of England from William the Conqueror to Elizabeth II and her heir-apparent to the British throne. 1980. NPA.

The Garden Birds Collection of 25 thimbles was issued by the Franklin Mint, Franklin Center, PA. The birds are original drawings and each thimble has trim of 24 carat gold. 1979. NPA.

Patchwork Quilt Thimble Collection was issued by Thimble Collectors Club portraying 24 different traditional quilt patterns. Each thimble is stamped "Gerold Porzellan, Bavaria; made in West Germany." They are porcelain and embellished with 24 carat gold. 1986. NPA.

Porcelain Dolls of the World was issued by the Thimble Collector's Club of Norwalk, CT, representing 24 different countries and/or ethnic groups. 1986. NPA.

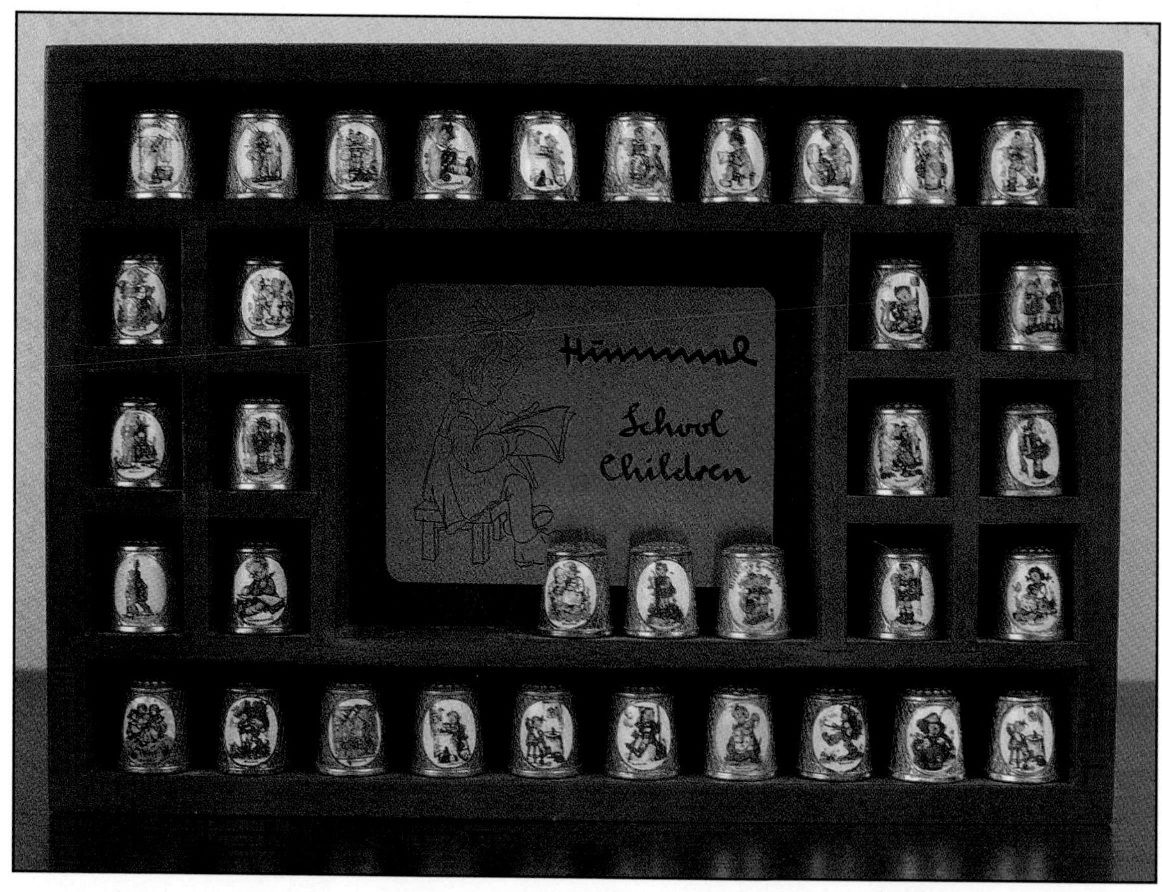

Hummel Collection Thimbles were issued by the Thimble Collectors Club, Norwalk, CT. The art work is by Sister M. I. Hummel and they were made in West Germany. The thimble surfaces were electroplated with silver and 22 carat gold. 1986. NPA.

Friends of Field and Forest was issued by Thimble Collectors Club of Norwalk, CT. The original paintings of the wildlife are by the renowned wildlife artist, Dick Twinney.
The thimbles are bone china manufactured by Oakley China in England. 1988. NPA.

Thimbles of the Far East were issued by Collectibles Ltd., Garden City, NY. This collection is particularly interesting because of the diversity of designs on the thimbles, each one is unique. 1984. NPA.

1st row:

1. USA; bird decorated sewing stand, hand carved, thimble holder, brass thimble, pincushion; c. 1910, $50.00.
2., 3. England; ebony, hand turned, 1994 reproductions of traditional designs, made by Guy Ravine, Weedom, Northampton; $65.00 – 75.00.
4. West Germany; "Golden Egg," egg and thimble, etched brass, plated 22 carat gold, background burnished, handmade, trimmed, and polished, inside velvet, thimble rim decorated with pearls; egg including base 9cm x 5cm; c. 1985, $400.00.
5. Small gold fill bird pincushion and thimble holder. $50.00.

2nd row:

1. Japan; glazed china, bucket thimble holder; c. 1920, $35.00.
2. USA; class project, handmade, painted; c. 1930, $10.00.
3. England; yew (same information 1st row 2., 3.), $50.00.

Thimble Holders

1st row:

1. USA; Louisville, KY, jeweler's paper thimble box, Simons Bros. sterling thimble; c. 1920, $75.00.
2. USA; Webster Co. sterling; c. 1900, $95.00.
3. USA; Tiffany & Co, New York, NY, acorn sterling and gold over sterling top; $350.00.
4. USA; Chas F. Schlegel Jeweler, Chillicothe, Ohio, velour and velvet thimble box, Simons Bros Co, 14 carat gold thimble; c. 1890, $250.00.
5. London, England; silversmith, J. Massey, sewing egg, sterling, unusual screw top for the period, beautiful designs; c. 1780, $650.00.
6. USA; Simons Bros. Co., tankard-style, sterling thimble; c. 1915, $200.00.
7. England; jewelry store thimble box, D&G Griffith, Hirwaen House, Pwllheli; thimble: Charles Horner maker, sterling; c. 1915, $95.00.

2nd row:

1. Exeter, England; leather thimble box containing sterling thimble; c. 1890, $65.00. (These boxes are now being reproduced and when available are $5.00 – 10.00, without thimble and made of composition material.)
2. England; velvet case with silver fittings, purple silk lining, Dorcas thimble; c. 1890, $175.00.
3. England; thimble bucket on chain, 14 carat gold over silver with enameled flowers; c. 1890, $125.00.

4., 5. England; thimble holder with chain, floral design, pressed brass sheet metal lined with velvet; c. 1890, $65.00 – 75.00.

3rd row:

1. England; leather box with brass fittings, velvet lining, English brass thimble; c. 1890, $75.00.
2. England; "A present from Rothesay," velvet lining, brass fittings, no maker's mark on silver thimble; c. 1900, $75.00.

Thimble Holder

London, England; original leather box and thimble, John Neal, watchmaker and silversmith to the Queen, Edgware Rd, lower half of the thimble design intertwined with shafts of wheat.

Thimble Holders

1st row:

1. Asia; vegetable ivory with matching thimble; c. 1890, $125.00.
2. USA; hand-carved wood, man and pig, brass thimble; c. 1920, $40.00.
3. Treen, England; Stern Bros. sterling thimble; c. 1910, $65.00.
4. England; walnut, hand carved, brass thimble; c. 1880, $65.00.
5. Asia; vegetable ivory holder and thimble; c. 1890, $85.00.

2nd row:

1. England; walnut carved acron shape; c. 1900, $60.00.
2. England; yew wood, acorn-shape holder; c. 1875, $45.00.
3. Kentucky, USA; wishbone thimble holder, cotton crochet with a chicken wishbone as a stay, used sometimes as a holiday ornament, handmade; c. 1910, $40.00.
4. USA; egg shape, maple; c. 1900, $45.00.
5. England; vegetable ivory, sterling thimble; c. 1900, $75.00.

3rd row:

1. USA; sweet grass holder, nickel-plated thimble; c. 1910, $50.00.
2., 3. England; transfer ware; c. 1890, $80.00 – 110.00.
   2. Velvet lining, scene of St. Petersburg, Florida.
   3. Scene of Shady Glen Falls and Devil's Oven, Catskill Mountains, New York.

Thimble Accessories

1st row:

1. England; boat thimble holder, clamshell base and hull, mother-of-pearl sails, brass riggings and brass thimble; c. 1880, $70.00.
2. France; boat thimble holder and pincushion; mother-of-pearl hull and sails, silver riggings, holder, cushion, and anchor, "souvenir of Calais"; c. 1880, $180.00.
3. USA; boy eating watermelon figural thimble and spindle for thread, Miller Silver Co., 14 carat thimble, no maker's mark; c. 1900, $325.00.

2nd row:

1. Germany; bear holding thimble and carrying pincushion, wood; c. 1880, $95.00.
2. Germany; glass slipper, painted, silver thimble with black stone cap; c. 1900, $90.00.

3rd row:

1. England; owl, bog oak with glass eyes, brass thimble; c. 1880, $60.00.
2. China; shell, carved ivory, thimble holder and pin tray, thimble, Ketcham & McDougal, sterling; c. 1875, $400.00.
3. Germany; man with head thrown back; carved, painted wood; brass thimble; c. 1900, $55.00.
4. Germany; standing bear, carved wood, brass thimble; c. 1880, $75.00.
5. France; sailboat; mother of pearl; silver riggings, thimble, and holder; c. 1880, $175.00.

4th row:

1. England; shoe, hand-carved wood, brass thimble; c. 1900, $50.00.

5th row:

1. England; Dickensesque character; silver over pewter, sterling thimble is the top hat; c. 1880, $175.00.
2. England; walnut and hummingbird on branch; pot metal, painted, walnut lined with velvet; sterling thimble; c. 1875, $295.00.
3. Germany; sitting bear, carved wood, brass thimble; c. 1880, $60.00.
4. Asia; barrel, dyed ivory, etched design; c. 1875, $70.00.

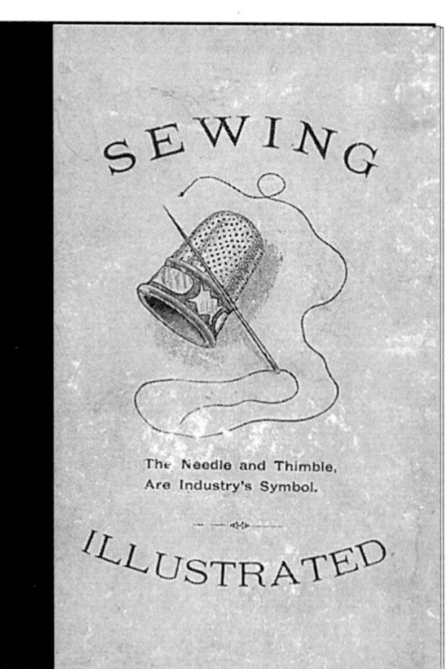

TABLE OF CONTENTS.

Sewing Illustrated. Sewing primer with songs and music for schools and families. Arranged by Louise J. Kirkwood, New York. American Book Co. Copyright, 1909.

A SEWING PRIMER,

WITH

Songs and Music.

PREPARATIONS FOR SEWING.

1. *How should a little girl be prepared for sewing?*
By having clean hands, clean nails, a clean face, tidy hair and a clean apron.

2. *On what should she sit while sewing?*
On a low seat.

3. *Why?*
That her feet may touch the floor, and her lap be level, so that her work will not slip off easily.

4. *Should she stoop over her work?*
No, because it cramps the lungs. She should bring her work to her eyes, rather than her eyes to her work.

THE WORKBASKET.

5. *What does a good sewer's workbasket contain?*
A thimble, pin cushion, needle book, with sewing needles, darning needles and a tape needle, scissors,

CUTTING. 11

an emery bag, and a bag or box to hold spools of cotton.

6. *What is the use of an emery bag?*
To brighten the needle when damp or rusty.

CUTTING.*

7. *What articles are needed for convenience in cutting?*
A table or lap-board to lay the material on, pins to fasten the pattern to it, and a good pair of scissors.

8. *How should you hold the scissors?*
With the pointed side downward.

9. *Which part of a plain calico dress waist should you cut first?*
The lining.

10. *Should you fold the cloth?*
Yes; double it evenly the lengthwise of the cloth.

11. *Why should you double it?*
So that where there are two pieces to be cut alike they may be cut together. This will also prevent the mistake of making them both for one side.

12. *How should you lay on the pattern?*
With the straight side of the pattern to the straight folded edges of the goods.

13. *How should you cut?*
Smoothly and evenly, so that the edges are not jagged.

* This is the natural place for this chapter, although the untrained child should not be expected to cut out her own work. She may have lessons in the use of the scissors, and be practiced in straight, bias, and curved cuts, on bits of calico or muslin. Since the Sewing Primer was prepared the School Sewing Practice Cloth has been designed, the use of which provides for the first lessons in cutting.

16 HEMMING.

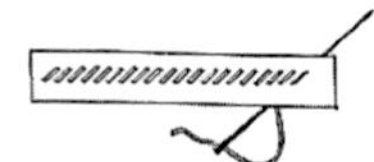

Showing the stitches on the right side of hem, with the needle in position.

HEMMING.

39. *How should a hem be turned down?*
Very evenly.

40. *How may a child learn to turn down a hem?*
By practicing on small squares or strips of soft paper.

41. *How should a sewer begin to hem?*
When the hem is turned down nicely she should turn the needle with the point toward the right, and stick it only through the edge turned down, leaving a little end of the thread to tuck under the hem, to be sewed under by the next stitches.

42. *How should she direct the needle when the hem is begun?*
Nearly on a line with the hem, with the point toward the left hand.

43. *Should the stitches be straight with the hem, or slanting?*
Slanting.

RUNNING—FELLING. 17

44. *How may a broad hem be kept even?*
By measuring every few inches with a paper measure.

45. *How should the ends of a hem be finished?*
They should be neatly over-handed.

RUNNING.

Showing running stitches, with the needle in position.

46. *What is the rule for fine running?*
Take up two threads and skip two.

FELLING.*

A fell seam, showing the first line of sewing finished, the edges turned under and partly hemmed.

47. *How must a fell seam be basted and sewed?*
With one edge of the garment above the other and

* See Song—*Try, O Try*, page 34.

THE PATCHWORK QUILT. 29

THE PATCHWORK QUILT.

O Mary made a patchwork quilt, oho, oho,
O Mary made a patchwork quilt, oho, oho,
Of prettiest colors it is made,
And in the prettiest pattern laid,
And oh how gay is Mary's patchwork quilt!

O Mary's quilt is soft and warm, oho, oho,
O Mary's quilt is soft and warm, oho, oho,
All lined with cotton fleecy white,
To keep the cold out well at night,
And oh how gay is Mary's patchwork quilt!

The girls who learn to knit and sew, oho, oho,
The girls who learn to knit and sew, oho, oho,
Will make the household warm and bright,
And fill the home with cheer and light,
And oh how gay is Mary's patchwork quilt!

SWIFT FLYING NEEDLE. 41

SWIFT FLYING NEEDLE.

O swift flying needle,
Stitching to song,
Through muslin and linen,
Speed you along.
So much is to do,
Quick you must be,
Work shall be well done
By you and by me.

Fingers so snowy white,
Daintily clean;
Stitches so small and light,
Scarcely are seen.
Over and under
The thread we will take,
Running and felling
The garments we make.

One little rule
Must ne'er be forgot:
Hide like a secret
Each little knot.
Thus active and lively
At work and at play,
We must grow wiser
And better each day.

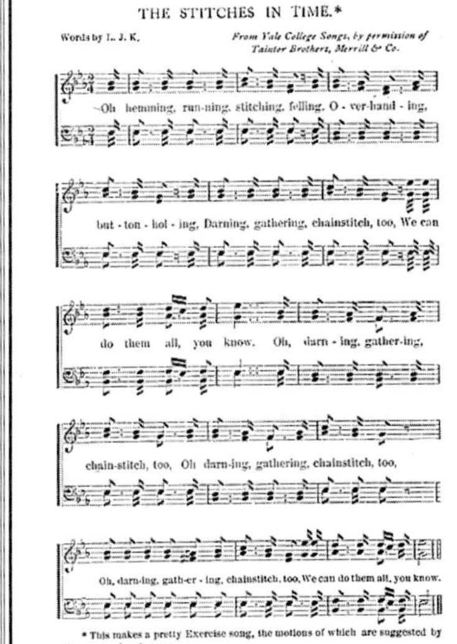

"THE STITCHES IN TIME." 51

"THE STITCHES IN TIME."

O hemming, running, stitching, felling,
Overhanding, buttonholing,
Darning, gathering, chainstitch too,
We can do them all, you know.

Now see how swiftly our needles fly,
First set low, then lifted high;
In and out how quick they go,
Shining brightly as they sew.

Fine twisted thread, you haste along
Binding piece to piece so strong,
Who can guess where you began,
Or the ending find, who can?

Neatly, lightly, swiftly sew,
Clicking softly as you go.
Shining needle, none shall be
Ever better friends than we.

Dutch or Flemish; drawing of a skillful needle woman; c. 1775, $110.00.

Chicago, USA; Boye thimble display, thread cutters, nickel-plated thimbles, painted tin display rack; c. 1930, $150.00.

Chapter Three

Chatelaines and Accessories

This chapter includes examples of chatelaines that were not exclusively designed for sewing. There are only three chatelaines pictured (page 64, #2) that have their original pieces. This is not uncommon, as there were probably many reasons (loss, wear, change of activity) that would require the original pieces of a chatelaine to be replaced. As is the case with most fine jewelry, the pieces of an exquisitely crafted chatelaine could also become separated. The interest in collecting fine chatelaines has increased and examples that have original chains and pieces are, of course, more costly.

Waist-hung items have been identified in artifacts that date to 2000 BC. The waist-hung chatelaine dates from 427 – 721 AD. The earliest recorded information on the "true chatelaine" is found in the April 1828 issue of "The World of Fashion." The January 1829 edition of the same periodical states that chatelaines "are a very expensive article of jewelry," describing examples that were decorated with gold buckles and chains. Interestingly, the cut steel chatelaines of the late eighteenth century were superior in terms of workmanship and beauty of design when compared to the mass produced, utilitarian chatelaines of the mid and late nineteenth century. The chains were made of different metals, fabrics, yarns, and leathers. As clothing styles began to change in the late 1800s, a chatelaine with a finger ring was introduced. They were often worn, but sometimes were looped over a dress or suit belt.

Chatelaine accessories are numerous and have a variety of purposes. Economic climate, styles, and trends dictated the function and design of the accessories. The craftsmen, artists, scribes (letter writers), tailors, nannies, nurses, and ladies of the house carried their tools on a belt clip with chains, the number of chains dictated by the requirements of their profession. Chatelaines, their practical function, and intricate beauty provide a fascinating study that seems to have no end.

England; gold plate, four chains; buttonhook, four page tablet, one empty chain, small waist clip medallion and a filigree medallion with one chain; when attached to a belt this has a draped effect; c. 1875, $600.00.

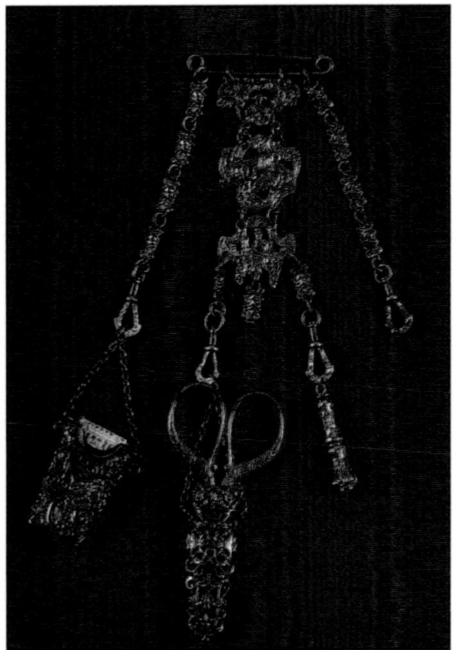

Right to left:
England, gold over sterling, four chains with a wax seal, scissors and sheath, and needle packet; large gold pin; c. 1888, $900.00.

Right to left:

1. England; sterling belt clip and chains with a Hallmark Birmingham 1900, "LE" maker's mark; four pieces, sterling needlecase with hallmark Birmingham 1917, maker's mark "JT&S," silver plate tablet with paper and pencil, sterling thimble holder with post, maker Foster and Bailey USA, needle case, sterling; c. 1890; $700.00.

2. England; silver plate filigree, with the exception of the scissors and thimble, it is original; five pieces, round pencil case with pencil, sheath and scissors, thimble bucket, thimble hallmark of London, sterling 1907, Charles Mappin maker, tablet with three ivory pages, pin safe shaped like a book marked "Scott Vol. I"; c. 1895, $800.00.

3. England; belt clip and chains have a hallmark of London, sterling, 1894, S. Mordan & Co.; three pieces, sterling spring action tape; polished metal scissors in sterling sheath with a hallmark of London 1894 with duty mark, sterling needlecase, $750.00.

Right to left:

1. England; sterling belt clip with ram's head on each side with rings for sterling chains, hallmark 1880, "930" stamp; two pieces, retractable button hook with hallmark sterling, Birmingham, 1890; silver filigree pomander; c. 1900, $250.00.
2. England; silver belt clip and five chains; five pieces, ladies sterling combo knife and glove hook, bird-handle clothing button hook, sterling silver tablet with celluloid pages, sterling silver pencil with hallmark Birmingham 1903, and silver mirror, the cover swings to one side; c. 1900, $650.00.
3. England; sterling belt clip and four chains; four pieces, sterling, velvet lined thimble holder with hallmark Birmingham, 1924, sterling thimble, sterling paper holder and pencil with hallmark London 1880 with a duty mark, mirror with hallmark sterling, maker's mark "HM," sterling tape measure with hand winder and silk tape with hallmark Birmingham 1903; $800.00.

1st row:

1. England; sterling silver chatelaine pin; c. 1880, $125.00.
2. England; sterling silver match or needle holder, it has a half circle opening in the back; c. 1880, $75.00.
3. England; silver plate, one chain with writing tablet and pencil, above the stag's head in the medallion are the words "THE CALL," belt clip; c. 1880, $125.00.
4. England; brass three slot pencil holder with a small stone in top of each pencil, the set is part of a small sketching case, the stone color represents the color in the drawing pencils; c. 1905, $50.00.
5. England; silver plate over brass, belt clip, no accessories; c. 1880, $350.00.

2nd row:

1. USA; sterling thimble holder with post, Webster Company; c. 1905, $75.00.
2. USA; sterling thimble holder with post, Webster Company; c. 1910, $95.00.

3rd row:

1. USA; sterling needle holder with chain; c. 1900, $45.00.
   (Needle holders of this style have been reproduced, high quality, but take care if what you want is an old piece.)
2. England; sterling handled scissors and sterling sheath, the blades of the scissors made in Germany; c. 1890, $110.00.

Germany; silver ring with six chains and tools, knife with blade, scissors, and nail tool, mesh coin purse, flat needle and pin case, double mirror, round pencil, notebook, marked "800" with Reich mark; c. 1900, $500.00–$700.00.

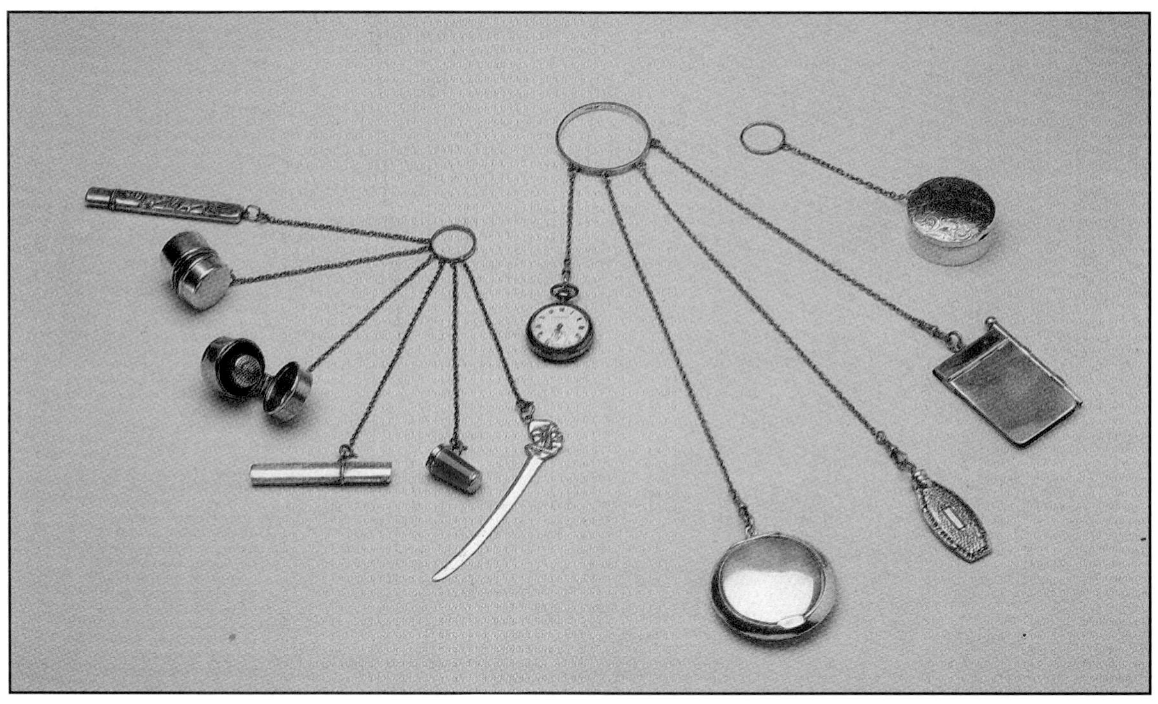

1. USA; sterling, six chain, finger ring chatelaine, pencil with dachshunds embossed on both sides, pincushion, thimble holder with thimble, needle case, French enameled cigarette holder and case, sterling letter opener; c, 1900, $325.00.
2. USA; "st. silver," finger ring with four chains, ladies watch, maker Q té Salter, second hand shape of a dagger with Art Nouveau female torso as handle, enameled diamond-shape in hour hand, two hands 10 carat gold, Roman numerals with decorative gold dots around the edge of face, Birmingham, sterling compact with mirror, vinaigrette or perfume screw top hammered silver, Birmingham, sterling tablet and pencil, each chain clasp marked "stig-sil"; c. 1900, $750.00.
3. USA; sterling nécessaire ring chatelaine, "JBco," used for carrying sewing or toilet items; c. 1900, $75.00–$125.00.

1. England; marked "coin silver"; two parts, top has a belt clip, a ring for chain and a yarn hook, second has a clip for hanging an accessory; c. 1870, $200.00.
2. USA; silver, heart-shaped decorative clip, two chains holding perfume with screw top; c. 1880, $125.00.
3. Europe; two-clip chatelaine that drapes, mother-of-pearl clip mounted on silver with applied decorative silver, small clip above glass perfume with decorative silver; c.1875, $700.00.
4. England; dance card with celluloid pages, embossed silver cover, gilt 24" chain and back; c. 1890, $250.00.

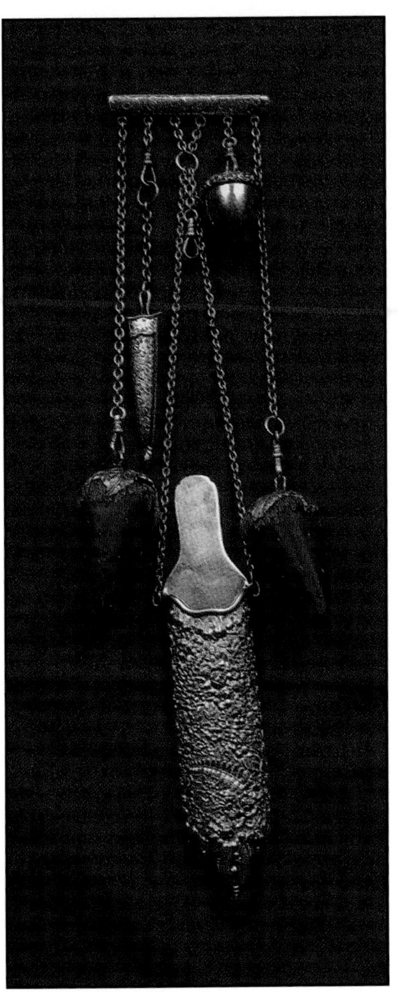

USA; five chain sterling chatelaine, Tiffany and Co., the bar pin is embossed "Mary V. Miller," two strawberry emeries with figural cloth caps, small two-part case, repousse eyeglasses case or scissors sheath, and an acorn thimble holder; c. 1907, $2,400.00.

England; sterling silver knitter's chatelaine, the cornucopia opens to become a pair of knitting needle guards, the hook just below the medallion belt clip holds the ball of yarn; c.1875, NPA.

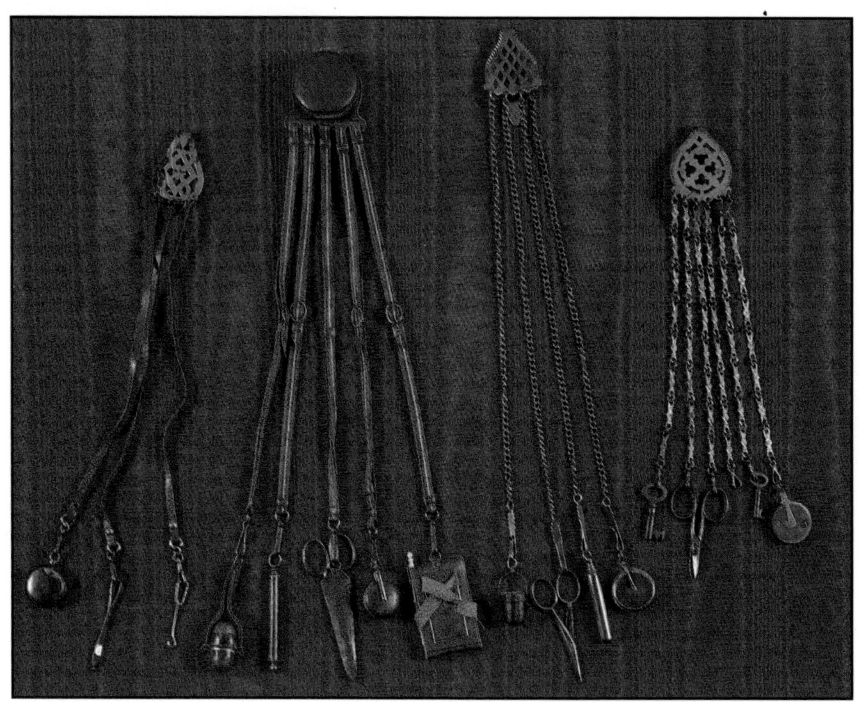

Left to right:

1., 3., 4. England; cut steel belt clips and accessories; c. 1865.

1. Three leather thongs and steel cut pieces, pin safe, clothing button hook, glove button hook; $275.00.

3. Four chains and pieces, thimble bucket, scissors, needle holder, pin safe; $750.00.

4. Five chains and four pieces, key, scissors, empty chain, key, and pin safe; $300.00.

2. England; gilded trim dyed leather; belt clip with coin purse; thimble holder with brass thimble, screw top needle holder, scissors with sheath, pin safe, tablet with ivory pencil, silk ribbon; c. 1900, $1,050.00.

England; medallion belt clip; brass two-piece embossed pin safe; sheath for scissors; c. 1890, $175.00.

Scotland; buttonhook, hallmark Edinburgh, sterling, 1872–73, the mounting is a thistle design with amber quartz blossom; 1¾"; $250.00. This is an excellent example of a silversmith taking a utilitarian tool and making it into a piece of jewelry.

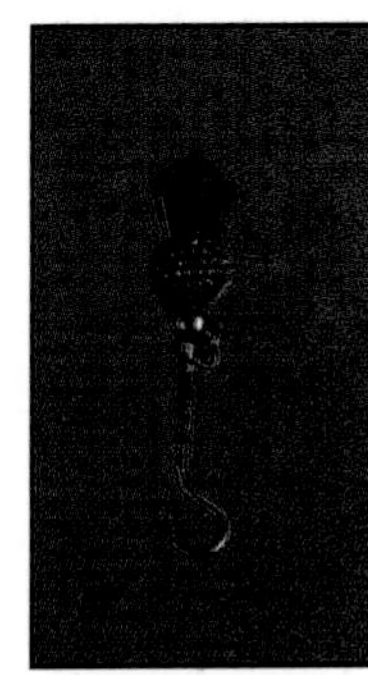

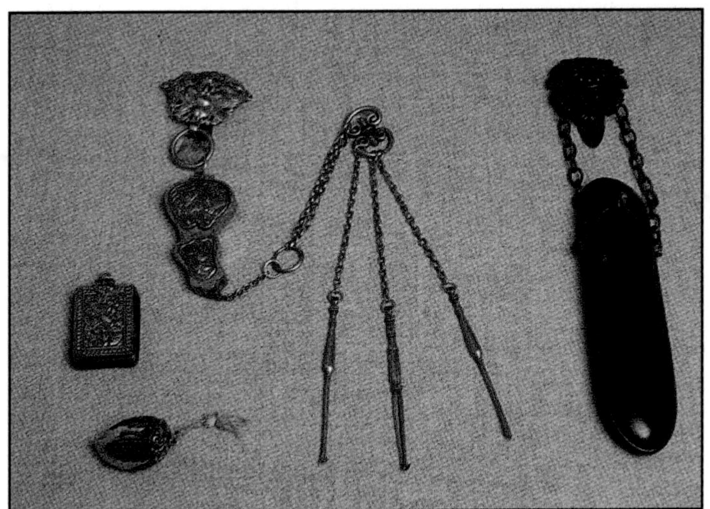

Accessories:

1. England; brass, pin safe; c. 1890, $65.00.
2. USA; pink silk rose bud with embroidery, sterling cap, silk tassel, emery; c. 1910, $75.00.

Chatelaines:

3. China; man's personal chatelaine, coin silver, maker's mark in Chinese characters; wax spoon, tweezers, toothpick; c. 1875, $900.00.
4. England; spectacle chatelaine with glasses, metal rosette waist clip and chains; c. 1900, $95.00–$125.00.

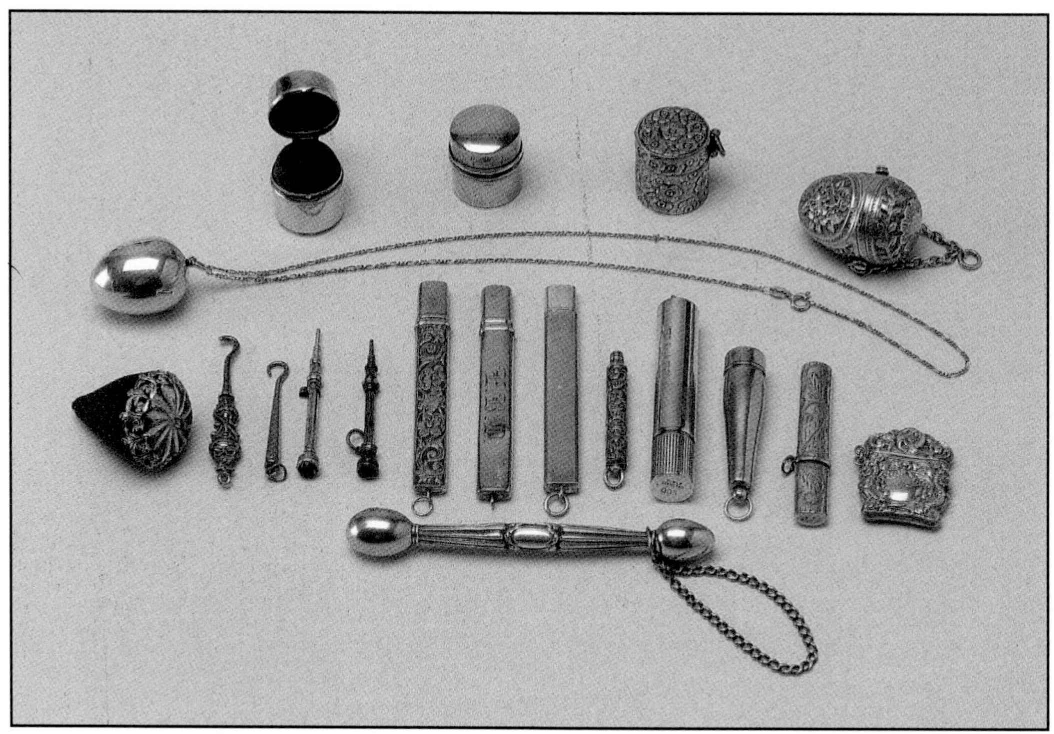

1st row:

1., 2. USA; sterling pincushion and thimble holder, Webster Co; c. 1910, $75.00 each.
3. Taiwan, ROC; sterling thimble holder; this is a quality reproduction of a traditional holder and decorative flower pattern; 1985, $25.00 – $35.00.
4. England; sterling thimble holder, with chain, beautiful craftsmanship of the Georgian period, hallmark Birmingham 1810, duty mark; $750.00.

2nd row:

1. USA; sterling egg thimble holder and chain, mark "Tiffany Co," "sterling"; $600.00.

3rd row:

1. USA; sterling cap strawberry emery; c. 1915, $110.00.
2. USA; sterling buttonhook, decorative handle; c. 1910, $30.00.
3. England; 10 carat gold glove hook; c. 1890, $40.00.
4., 5. England; sterling pencils with glass caps; c. 1890, $45.00 each.
6.– 8. England; sterling flat pencils; c. 1900, $45.00 – $65.00.
9. England; sterling pencil; c. 1890, $30.00.
10. USA; sterling needle holder, Towle Silversmith; c. 1925, $45.00.
11. USA; sterling needle holder, c. 1915, $25.00.
12. Sterling needle holder, reproduction of traditional style, shape, and surface design; c. 1990, $15.00 – $20.00.
13. USA; sterling stamp holder; c. 1900, $130.00.

4th row:

1. USA; sterling glove darner with chain; c. 1900, $90.00.

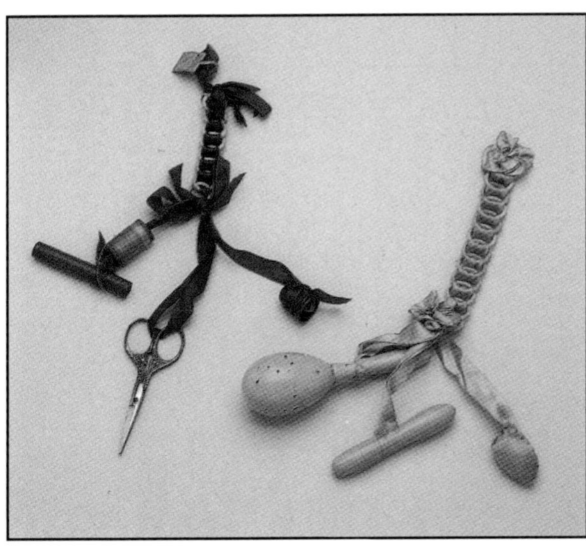

1. USA; ribbon and ring chatelaine, John Taylor Dry Goods Co. price tag, date 7-3-25, items include thread, wood needle case, scissors, English brass thimble; 7"; 1925, $35.00.
2. USA; silk ribbon and ring chatelaine, items include small sock darner, small mitten/glove darner, emery; 8"; c. 1920, $45.00.

Both chatelaines are attached to a lapel or waistband with a safety pin behind the rosette.

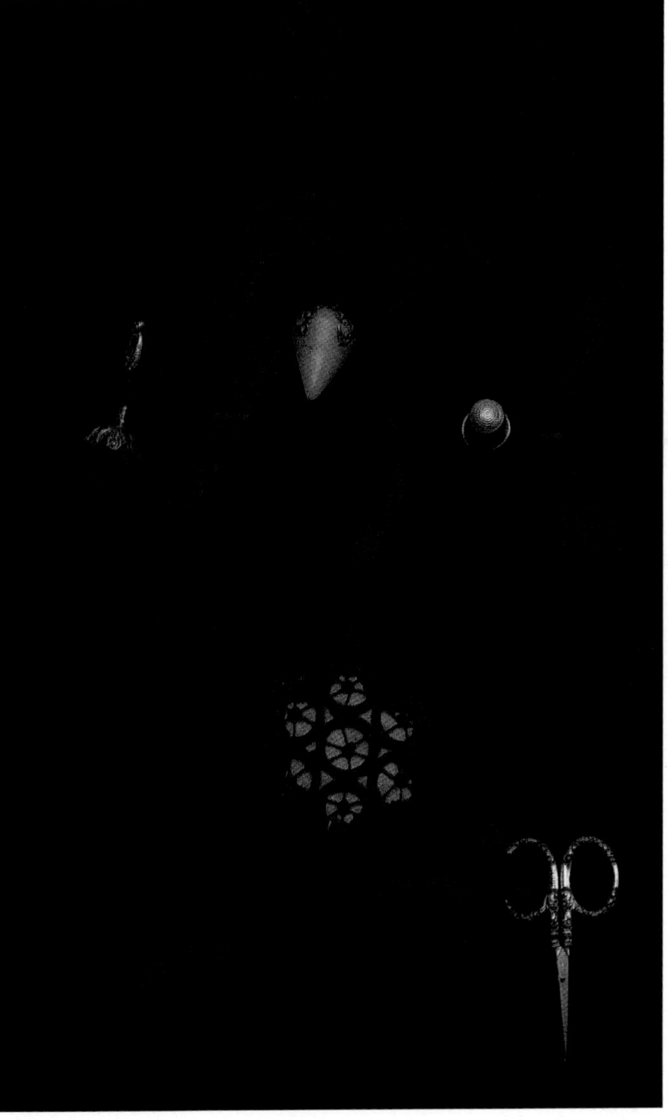

Ribbon chatelaine: This chatelaine is made up of silk ribbons with a handmade silk bag and beautiful crochet ring and web designs needlecase. The tools are commercially made. Left to right: sterling handled emery, sterling scissors, strawberry shaped beeswax with sterling cap, needle and pin case, and sterling thimble and its bag. The beautiful bow has a safety pin for attaching to a garment. This chatelaine came out of the Blythe family estate of Paducah, Kentucky. Exhibit in Victorian Quilt Show, 1994 — Museum of American Quilter's Society.

SOLID SILVER CHATELAINES, &c.

No. 22,230.
New Design, Richly Chased Chatelaine, with Safety Chain. £1 17 6

No. 22,232
NEW DESIGN, REGD. No. 315,537.
Solid Silver Chatelaine,
Seven Chains,
all Richly Chased Repoussé.
£2 12 6

No. 22,231.
New Design, Elaborately Chased and Pierced Chatelaine, with Safety Chain.
£2 0 0

No. 22,233.
Solid Silver-mounted Manicure Set, comprising 9 Instruments, 2 Boxes, and Nail Polisher, in Best Morocco Case, £4 12 6
Morocco Case, containing Nail Polisher, 1 Box, and 4 Instruments, £2 5 0

ILLUSTRATIONS AND PRICES
OF
GOLD CHATELAINES
ON APPLICATION.

No. 22,234.
Richly Chased Solid Silver-Mounted Manicure Set, consisting of 5 Instruments, in Best Morocco Case.
£2 5 0

Victorian Jewelry Portland House, 1891. Intro by Peter Kinks.

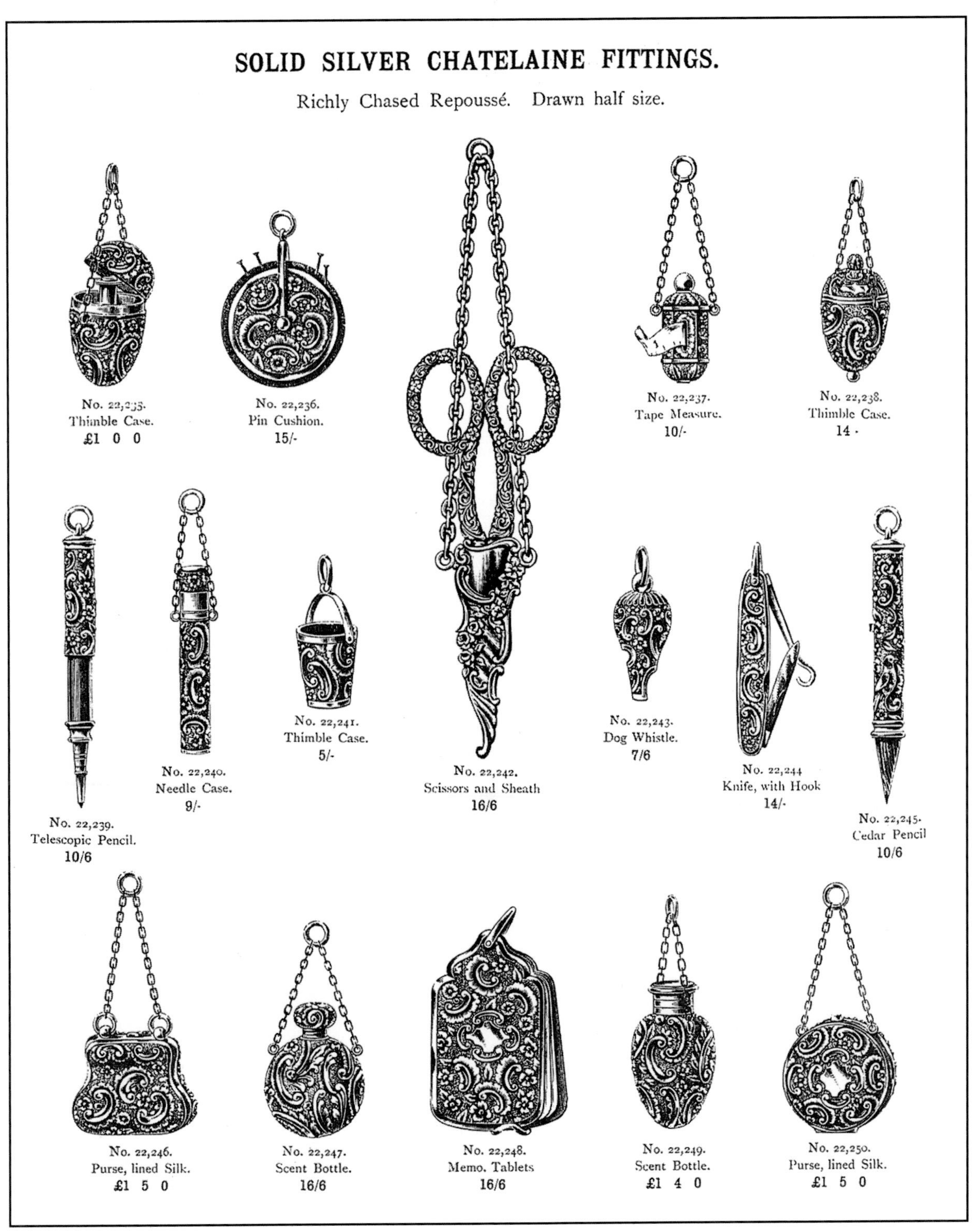

SOLID SILVER CHATELAINE FITTINGS.

Richly Chased Repoussé. Drawn half size.

No. 22,235.
Thimble Case.
£1 0 0

No. 22,236.
Pin Cushion.
15/-

No. 22,237.
Tape Measure.
10/-

No. 22,238.
Thimble Case.
14 -

No. 22,239.
Telescopic Pencil.
10/6

No. 22,240.
Needle Case.
9/-

No. 22,241.
Thimble Case.
5/-

No. 22,242.
Scissors and Sheath
16/6

No. 22,243.
Dog Whistle.
7/6

No. 22,244
Knife, with Hook
14/-

No. 22,245.
Cedar Pencil
10/6

No. 22,246.
Purse, lined Silk.
£1 5 0

No. 22,247.
Scent Bottle.
16/6

No. 22,248.
Memo. Tablets
16/6

No. 22,249.
Scent Bottle.
£1 4 0

No. 22,250.
Purse, lined Silk.
£1 5 0

Victorian Jewelry Portland House, 1891.

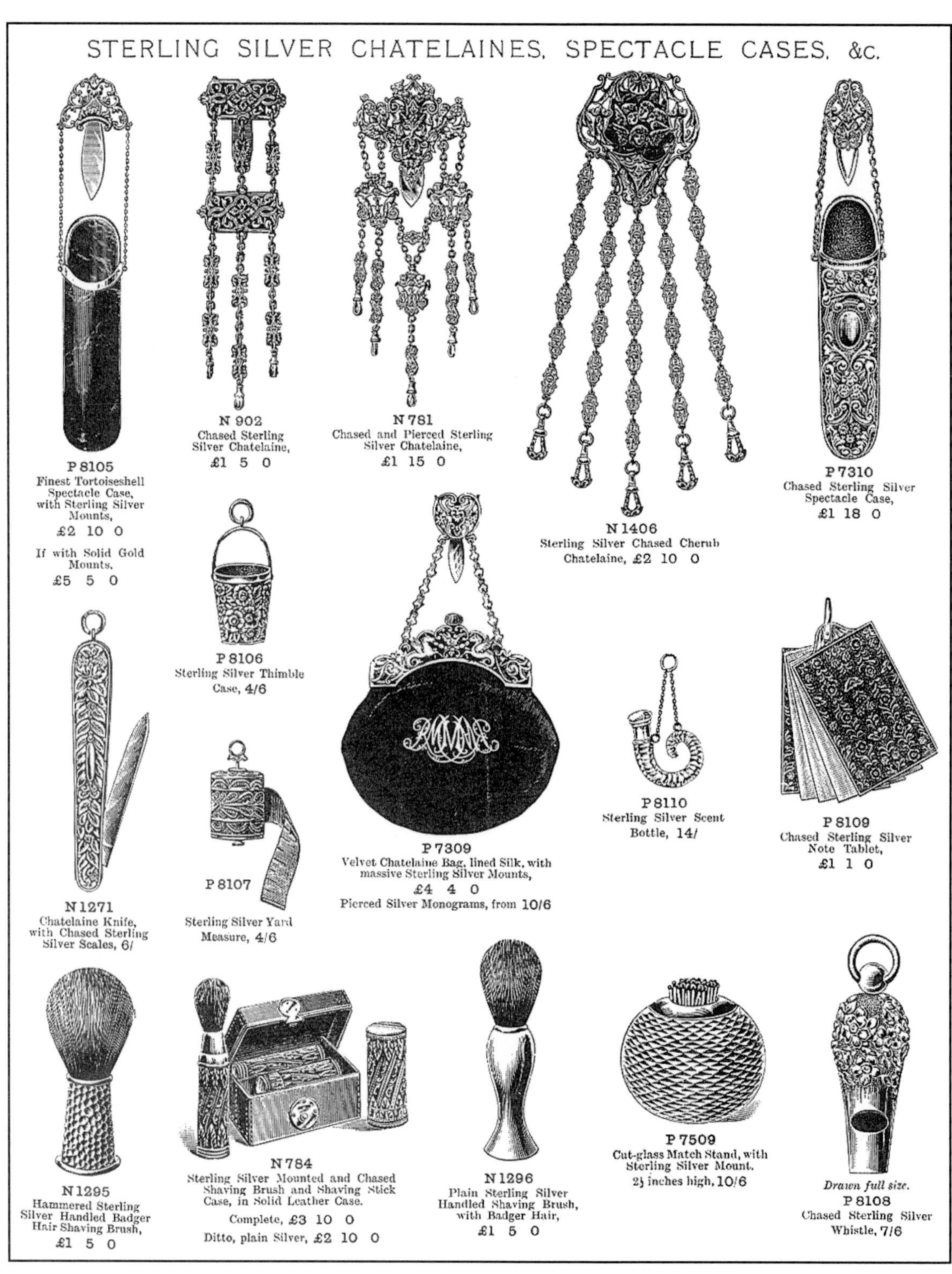

STERLING SILVER CHATELAINES, SPECTACLE CASES, &c.
P 8105
Finest Tortoiseshell Spectacle Case, with Sterling Silver Mounts,
£2 10 0
If with Solid Gold Mounts,
£5 5 0
N 902
Chased Sterling Silver Chatelaine,
£1 5 0
N 781
Chased and Pierced Sterling Silver Chatelaine,
£1 15 0
N 1406
Sterling Silver Chased Cherub Chatelaine, £2 10 0
P 7310
Chased Sterling Silver Spectacle Case,
£1 18 0
P 8106
Sterling Silver Thimble Case, 4/6
N 1271
Chatelaine Knife, with Chased Sterling Silver Scales, 6/
P 8107
Sterling Silver Yard Measure, 4/6
P 7309
Velvet Chatelaine Bag, lined Silk, with massive Sterling Silver Mounts,
£4 4 0
Pierced Silver Monograms, from 10/6
P 8110
Sterling Silver Scent Bottle, 14/
P 8109
Chased Sterling Silver Note Tablet,
£1 1 0
N 1295
Hammered Sterling Silver Handled Badger Hair Shaving Brush,
£1 5 0
N 784
Sterling Silver Mounted and Chased Shaving Brush and Shaving Stick Case, in Solid Leather Case.
Complete, £3 10 0
Ditto, plain Silver, £2 10 0
N 1296
Plain Sterling Silver Handled Shaving Brush, with Badger Hair,
£1 5 0
P 7509
Cut-glass Match Stand, with Sterling Silver Mount,
2½ inches high, 10/6
Drawn full size.
P 8108
Chased Sterling Silver Whistle, 7/6

Victorian Jewelry Portland House, 1891.

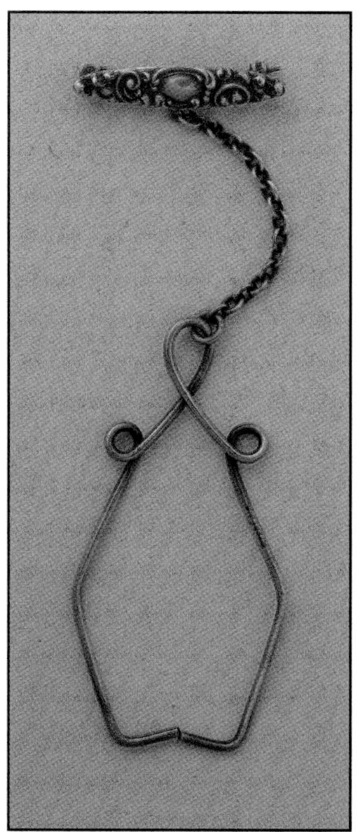

Lapel pin thread holder, used in sewing, crochet, and other continuous thread handwork projects. See page 121.

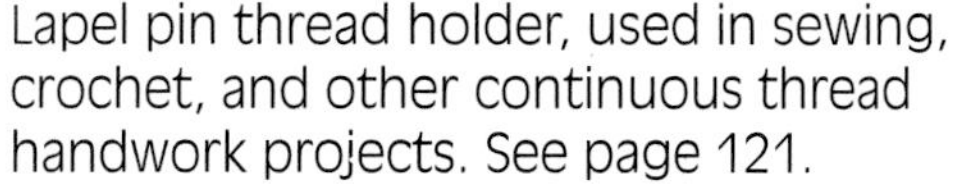

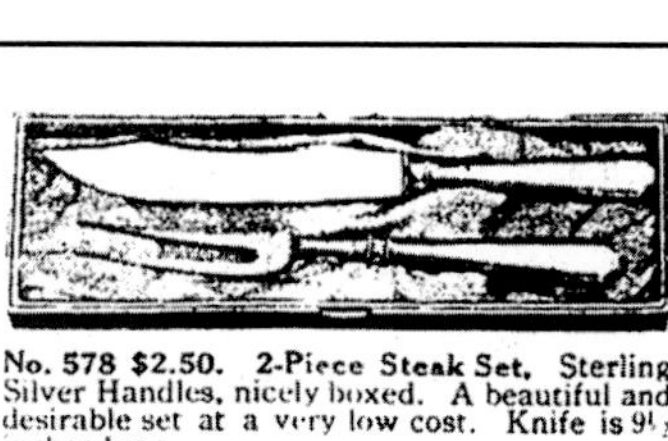

No. 578 $2.50. 2-Piece Steak Set, Sterling Silver Handles, nicely boxed. A beautiful and desirable set at a very low cost. Knife is 9½ inches long.

No. 306 $2.00. Solid 10K Gold Brooch set with sapphire. A very pretty design at a price that cannot be equalled.

No. 538 40c. 12 Assorted Holiday Correspondence cards, die stamped, with envelopes. For the above price we will stamp on the cards, any Old English Letter or two-letter monogram in blue, green, gold or silver ink.

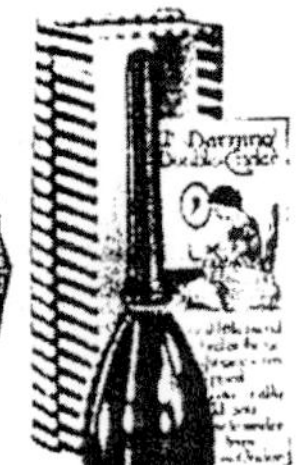

No. 594 35c. Mahogany Darner with Needles, with hand colored card in beautiful box. A convenient article for the work basket or an appropriate selection for a remembrance.

No. 579 $1.50. Cheese Plate and Server, Plate is cut with beautiful design, and is 6½ inches in diameter. Server has Sterling Silver handle in hammered design.

No. 572 $1.00. Spool Holder, Sterling Silver. Pins to the clothing. 1½ in. wide.

No. 569 85c. Shuttle of Sterling Silver. A nice token that is sure to be appreciated. Any name engraved free. 2¾ inches long.

No. 518 $2.00. Sewing Bag of Old Rose Silk, with one row of gold braid. A very handsome article. Bag is 6½ inches in diameter.

No. 595 85c. Pin Basket containing black-headed pins in the form of blackberries. A pleasing novelty that oftentimes will be of great service.

No. 505 $1.25 the pair. Solid Mahogany Candlesticks. A pair of these sticks with the shades shown in our catalog make very pretty ornaments. The sticks are 7½ inches high.

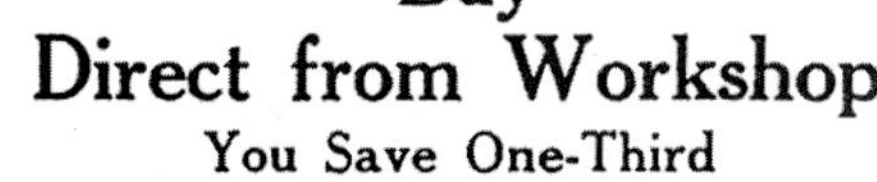

Buy Direct from Workshop

You Save One-Third

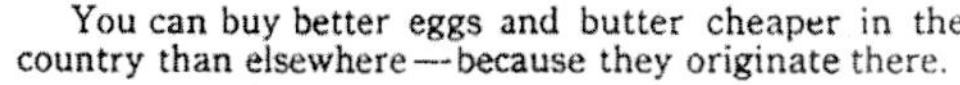

You can buy better eggs and butter cheaper in the country than elsewhere—because they originate there.

Likewise the latest gowns can be had for less money in the large cities, because it is there that styles are created and the goods manufactured.

Therefore, it is reasonable to assume that you can buy better jewelry and kindred lines cheaper from Providence, R. I., because Providence is the jewelry center of the world.

And the Baird-North Co. of Providence are the largest Mail Order Jewelers in the World.

Our catalog of jewelry, silverware and kindred lines, published annually with periodical supplements, is the most up-to-date and representative presentation ever issued.

Its 200 pages containing 10,000 articles of diamonds, watches, jewelry, leather goods, novelties, toiletware, tableware and associated lines, will suggest to you an appropriate gift for Christmas or any other occasion, or an article for yourself or your home.

And best of all YOU SAVE ONE-THIRD because you buy from the Workshop in the jewelry center of the world.

You take no chance and you do save money.

Every article is guaranteed to give you complete satisfaction or we will return your money. We guarantee free, safe and prompt delivery wherever you live.

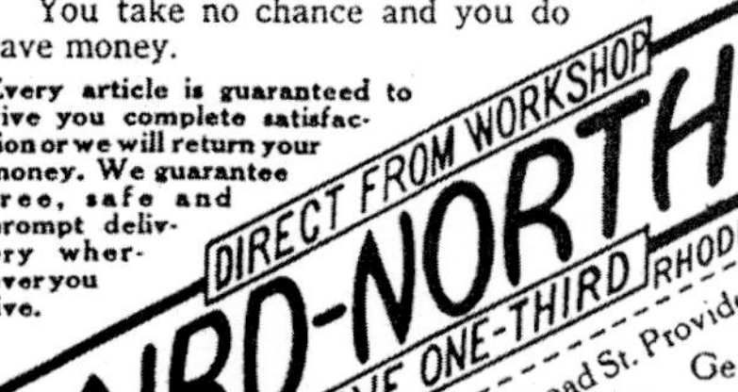

BAIRD-NORTH CO. 205 Broad St. Providence, R. I.

Gentlemen:
Please send me FREE without obligation, your 200 page catalog containing 10,000 articles of jewelry, silverware, novelties and gifts.

Name ______________________

Address ______________________

Home Needlework Magazine ad. October, 1916.

NEEDLECRAFT

MAY 1929 MAGAZINE TEN CENTS

Needlecraft Magazine, May, 1929.

Chapter Four

Sewing Kits, Boxes, and Baskets

The sewing kit has evolved from differing origins and has assumed many names. This small sewing essential is basically a portable container packed with whatever items the manufacturer determined were necessary and would fit in the designated space. The French emphasized the streamlined practicality of the sewing kit, calling it a necessaire. Often it was a large box containing many small boxes that held a variety of items. The German hussifs were topped with a thimble in order to secure the sewing items inside the small container. The English Lady's Companion first appeared in the late eighteenth century and gained popularity during the nineteenth century. The necessaire of choice for the continental woman after 1850 was a small handbag that contained a number of sewing tools. A variation of the hussif was manufactured in the United States and England after 1900. They were made of less expensive materials such as celluloid and aluminum and were often embellished with advertisements or a decorative band of paint or celluloid. Often, they were given away by a company or hotel and also as souvenirs (see bottom photograph on page 79).

Sewing boxes that were attractive and well made have been popular since the seventeenth century. Large numbers of boxes were produced in the south of Germany during the seventeenth century and sold throughout Europe. These boxes came in many sizes and had various decorations ranging from the simple to the ornate. Wood was the most common construction material for these boxes because of its availability, but some others were made of leather, mother-of-pearl, bone, ivory, and papier mache. The whimsical shell boxes with the excessive Victorian decoration were created as a result of the expansion of a railway system allowing travel to English coastal areas. These boxes were a natural for the souvenir industry, and it was not long before the shells and boxes were available at seaside and lake resorts throughout the world. Sewing boxes often have a pincushion and small, sentimental cut-out as a centerpiece on the top. Before decoration, the boxes were made of either wood or heavy paper and were often painted inside.

Even before recorded history, woven sewing baskets were in use. These baskets have a universal appeal and, depending on the creative ability of the individual, they range from utilitarian to artistic. Like the sewing boxes, sewing baskets often had a pincushion on top. The Chinese adorned them with beads and coins which were attached with a thin silk rope. Sweet grass was one of the materials commonly used to make the baskets, as well as split oak, poplar, cedar, and willow.

The "roll-up" or "housewife" is a sewing item used to store pins, needles, small scissors, and perhaps buttons. It is generally handmade from fabric. On page 80 there is an example that shows several that were made in Pennsylvania. Note the variety of fabrics as well as the different sizes and designs. The roll-up was often given to men who were leaving home for a long period of time. Sailors and prisoners of war made them as gifts (see page 80, row 3, #6).

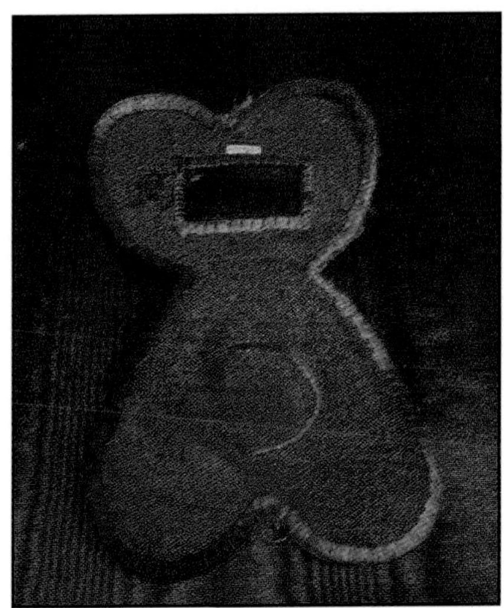

1. USA; Elizabethtown, KY, "housewife" made of gray wool fabric from a Confederate soldier's uniform, one pocket; c. 1865, $125.00.
2. "Housewife," open, red wool for needles and pins.

The housewife was made with fabrics on hand. Some fabrics were beautiful and others utilitarian. They were small and very portable. "Roll-up" is another name for small kits.

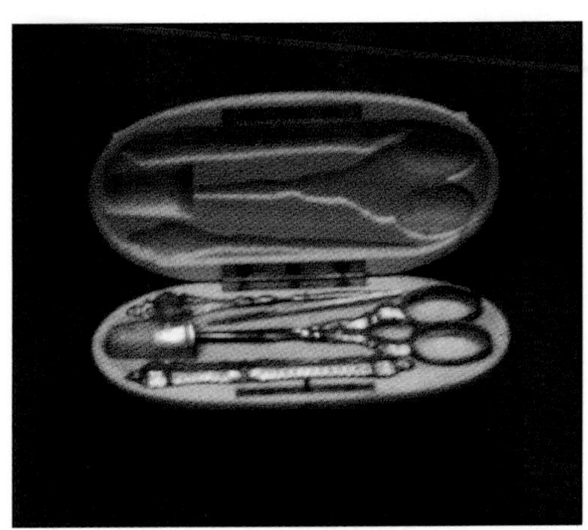

France; etui, ivory case, five pieces, gilt over sterling, scissors, stiletto, needlecase, thimble, bodkin, beautiful condition; c. 1860, $700.00 – 900.00.

Left top: England; wood spindle with winders and cylinder for needles; c. 1900, $50.00.
Lower: England; metal gilt walnut, felt lined, needles, pins, thread, and thimble; c. 1910, $45.00.
Right: Leather, embroidered pages for needles and pins, removable silk pin cushion, thimble holder, and sterling Webster thimble, one pocket; c. 1875, $300.00.

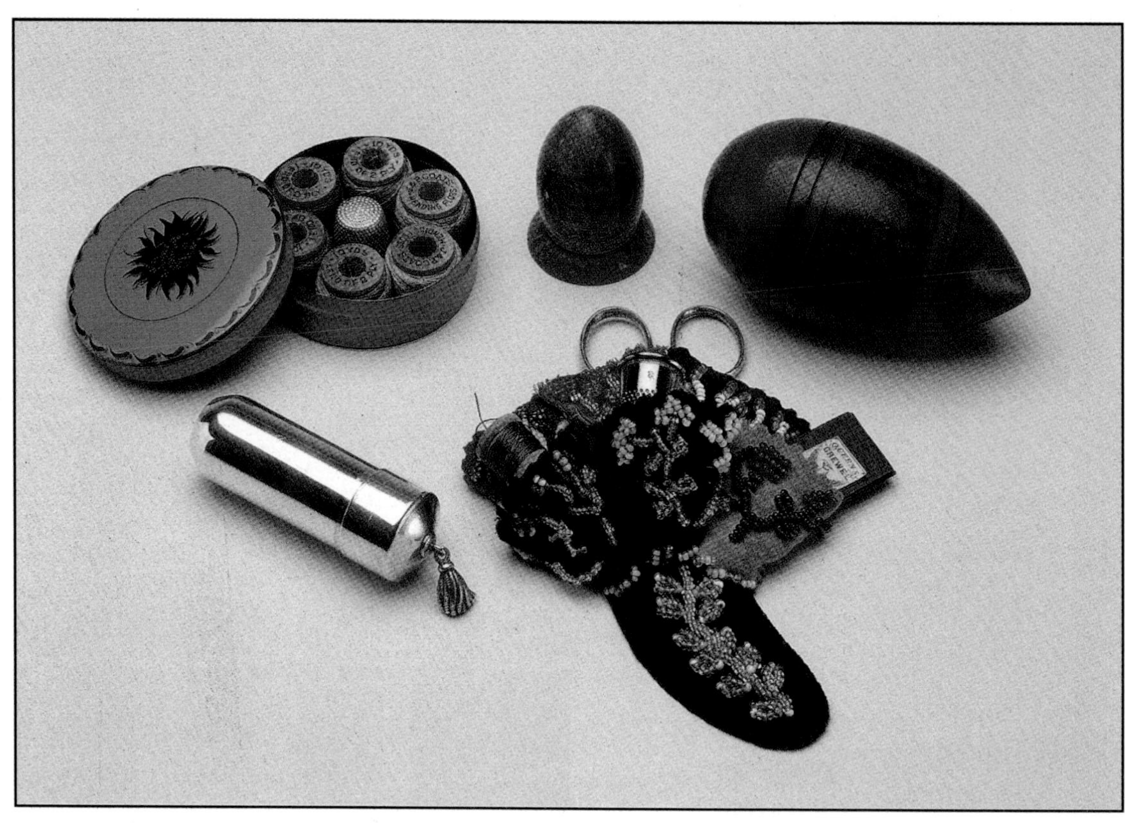

1st row:

1. USA; J. P. Coats darning kit with six spools darning thread, aluminum thimble, and two needles, painted; c. 1930, $40.00.
2. Germany; transfer ware, wood sewing kit (thread and needles), transfer reads "the fair maid's house Perth, made in Germany," there are needle scratches that would suggest that it was used as a darner; c. 1890, $70.00.
3. Germany; transfer ware, wood darning egg with needles, pins, thread, and thimble inside, transfer Bad Niendorf; c. 1900, $125.00.

2nd row:

1. USA; sterling, Tiffany and Co makers, "L"; the kit includes a cylinder for needles and three winders for thread, tassel-style decoration on top's ring; c.1920, $350.00.
2. England; velvet beaded posey kit for scissors, thread, thimble, and needles; c. 1875, $50.00.

1st row:

1. USA; celluloid with silver gilt design overlay, sewing kit with needle holder and thread; c. 1920, $30.00.
2. Germany; "Piccadilly," wood, combination sewing and needle case with thimble visible through the top; c. 1900, $50.00 – 65.00.
3. USA; wood, bullet shape with thimble, needle, and thread; $40.00.
   4. Painted green, decorated with flowers; c. 1915, $30.00 – 40.00.
5., 6. USA; metal, painted, military issue World War I, included thimble, thread, and needles with paper insert with directions on how to open the kit; c. 1915, $25.00 – 30.00.
7. Italy; natural wood, with varnish, thimble, needles, and thread on spindle; $45.00.
8. USA; plastic with needles and thread; $10.00.

2nd row:

1. USA; aluminum, paper line, needles, thread, and thimble; c. 1940, $12.00.
2. USA; gilt over metal, spindle with needles and thread; c. 1935, $20.00.
3. USA; metal egg, gilt top and flocked lower half; this is a New York World's Fair souvenir; top engraved "New York, The Empire State" with outlines of five state buildings and Statue of Liberty; inside is velvet lined with complete kit including needles, thread, thimble, also ½" glass medallion etched and painted with logo of the Fair and "1939 NYWF"; $250.00.
4. Germany; shoe with gilt stork scissors and thimble, label "1933 Century of Progress, Chicago," sole is stamped "D. Peres Germany," all original, mint condition; 1933, $225.00.
5. Germany; stamped on metal closure, marbleized paint; c. 1920, $12.00.
6. England; egg-shaped wood with matching wood thread winder; c. 1900, $75.00.

3rd row:

1. England; ivory, painted, silk tassel, thimble is the top, kit complete with spindle, thread on winder and cylinder with needles; c. 1890, $75.00.
2. Italy; celluloid, thimble is the hat, painted face, spindle for thread and needle case; label on bottom of stand "Genova, Hotel Britannia," souvenir; c. 1920, $95.00.
3. Egg gilt finish, kit complete, thread, needles, and thimble; c. 1915, $50.00 – 65.00.
4. USA; aluminum, "Order of the Easter Star" souvenir, thimble is top, complete kit inside; c. 1950, $20.00.
5. USA; silver plate, thimble is top, complete cylinder kit inside; c. 1920, $60.00
6. USA; sterling silver, complete with thimble, spindle with thread, needle case; c. 1930, $125.00.
7. England; brass, engraved, silk tassel, complete with thread and needles; c.1910, $65.00.

1st row:

1. USA; wood egg, a hole in small end for drawing thread from egg; c. 1900, $30.00.
2. USA; leather, scissors and sheath on top, snap top with wool pages for pins and needles, ribbon threaded from outside through spool openings; c. 1930, $50.00 – 65.00.
3. USA; cardboard box, Duro Bands (rubber bands), Stanley Home Products tape measure, six yards of lace, four spools sewing thread, patent medicine box of pins, one spool of Merrick darning thread, small scissors; typical "make-do" sewing box; c. 1940, $7.50.
4. England; yew wood, velvet cushion, sterling thimble, kit unscrews at center and contains thread; c. 1880, $60.00 – 75.00.
5. Germany; plastic, flocked liner, gilt stork scissors and thimble, label "Qualitat made in Solingen"; c. 1980. $25.00.
6. England; leather darning kit, gold lettering "Troubles are ended when they are mended," complete with thread and needles; c. 1915, $45.00.

2nd row:

1. USA; horn, screw top, needles and loose thread, brass thimble; c. 1900, $45.00.
2. USA; roll-up, tan leather with snap closure, painted metal ends, contains dark brown needle pocket for thread and thimble, lettering "Compliments of Hartsfield thru out California"; c. 1940, $25.00.

3rd row:

1. USA; sweet grass medallion; attached scissors with sheath and thimble in holder; velvet pincushion in basket attached to disc; c. 1890, $70.00.
2. USA; etui, cloth over cardboard, Maine; c. 1988, $65.00.
3. England; treated paper and gold lettering, five units including two for various needles, two with wool pages, and center for bodkin, scissors, two bodkins, and tapestry needle, lettering "R. J. Roberts, Patent Parabola Needles," "Made in England"; c. 1890, $55.00.
4. USA; paper fold over, Lydia Pinkham advertisement; c. 1935, $25.00.

4th row:

1. USA; machine-made petit point case, complete; c. 1950, $25.00.
2. England; enamel, four pieces, Metropolitan Museum of Art reproduction, Halcyon Days Enamel, needle case, pincushion, thimble, tape measure; c.1990. NPA.
3. USA; roll up, black leather, snap closure, thread and thimble; c. 1900, $5.00.

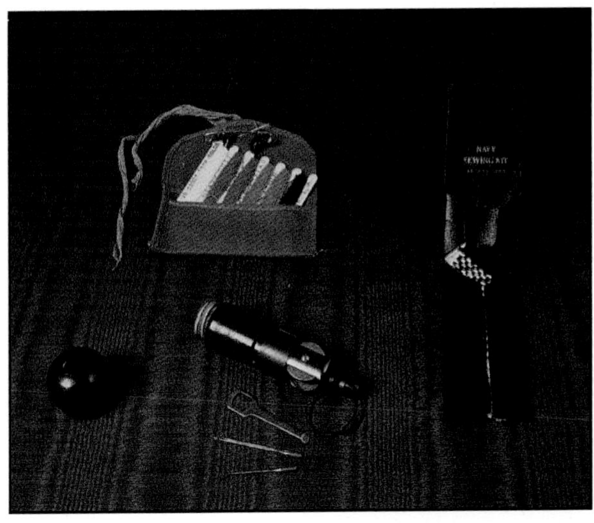

1st row:

1. USA; World War I US Army issue fabric sewing kit; needles, thread, and buttons; envelope folder with braid tie, olive green; c.1915, $25.00.
2. USA; Navy issue sewing kit; black leather, gold letters "U. S. Navy Sewing kit," needles and black and white thread; c.1930, $25.00.

2nd row:

1. USA; wooden case; leather sewing kit with sinew thread and tools; bottom unscrews with attachment storage, three pieces; c.1940, $10.00.

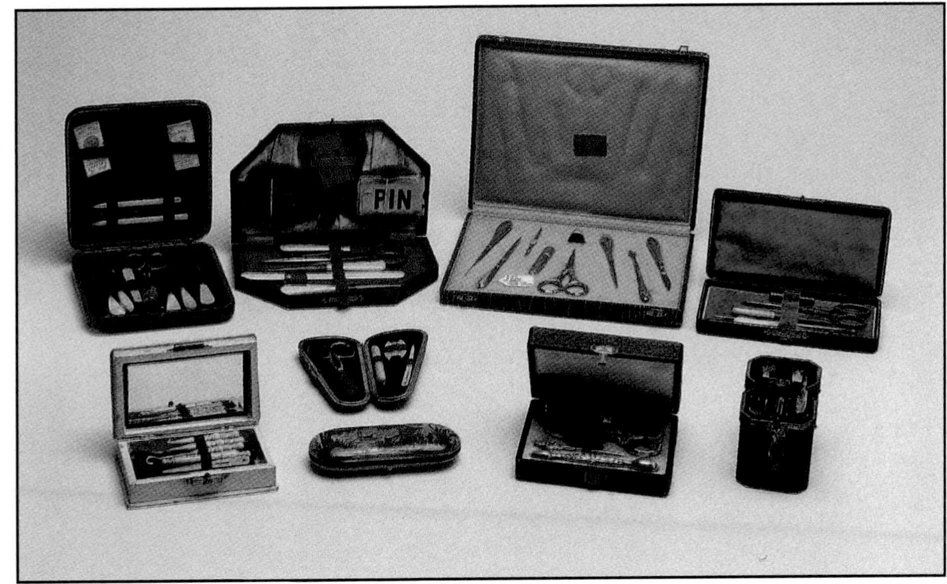

1st row:

1. England; leather box, eight mother-of-pearl pieces, steel scissors and bone bodkins, brass thimble, needle packets, velvet lining; c. 1890, $75.00.
2. England; leather box, four bone pieces, steel scissors and bodkins, silk lining; c.1890, $100.00.
3. France; sterling silver, nine pieces, excellent condition, silk lining; c.1910, $500.00.
4. England; leather box, silk lining, two ivory and four steel pieces; c.1880, $80.00.

2nd row:

1. England; snake skin-design leather, velvet lining, three ivory pieces, one steel piece, and one brass piece; c.1880, $125.00.

3rd row:

1. England; celluloid covered box with beveled mirror, cut steel fittings, six ivory tools; c. 1865, $100.00.
2. France; papier-mâché case, hand painted with Oriental scenes, signed on back "made in France," scissors and lles thimble; c. 1900, $190.00.
3. USA; leather covered box, silk lining, silver clasp, sterling glove darner, sterling scissors, sterling capped emery, sterling thimble; c.1875, $250.00.
4. England; "Lady's Companion" with cut steel fittings, four cut steel tools, one missing, mirror, needle packet; c.1850, $225.00.

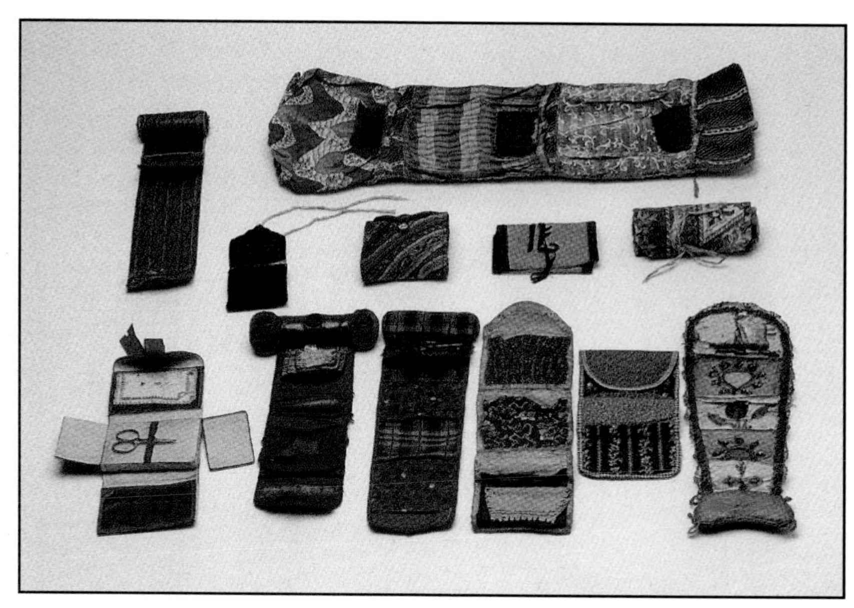

Roll-ups

1st row:

1. Pennsylvania; glazed chintz, red wool crepe for needles and ends of pincushion roll, one 2" x 3" pocket, one slotted pocket for four 9" knitting needles, hand sewn; 13½" x 3"; c. 1880, $65.00.
2. Pennsylvania; three pockets, five cotton prints, metal buttons, hand-sewn wool needle pages on each pocket, includes a note in pocket saying "this sewing case belonged to Deborah Jones Redue 1846–1940"; 24" x 7½"; c. 1870, $90.00.

2nd row:

1. – 4. Pennsylvania, hand sewn.
   1. Velvet, sacking pincushion; c. 1900, $15.00.
   2. Wool challis, linen lining, horse hair pincushion, wool pages for needles and pins, hand sewn, c. 1875, $55.00.
   3. Canvas, velvet lining and binding, hand sewn and embroidered, wool pages for needles and pins; c. 1900, $20.00.
   4. Cotton prints, bird print pockets, wool pages for needles and pins, hand sewn; c. 1860, $60.00.

3rd row:

1. England; green leather; one pocket, scissors, wool pages for needles and thread, hand sewn and embroidered; c.1900, $45.00.
2. – 5. Pennsylvania; hand sewn.
   2. Leather, silk lining, three pages for needle and pins, pincushion roll with thimble well and thimble, two pockets; c. 1880, $110.00.
   3. Wool challis, four pockets, four pages for needle and pins, pincushion roll; c.1890, $70.00.
   4. Cotton prints, silk lining, three pockets, three pages for needle and pins; c. 1875, $60.00.
   5. Cotton print, four pockets; c.1880, $25.00.
6. USA; New England; cover glazed cotton print, lined with paper then silk inside, top panel sailing ship with flag, heart with mirror missing, flower, mirror, pincushion, two sizes of silver wire as well as glass beads used for decorative work (it may have been a seaman's project while on a long voyage); c. 1840, $350.00.

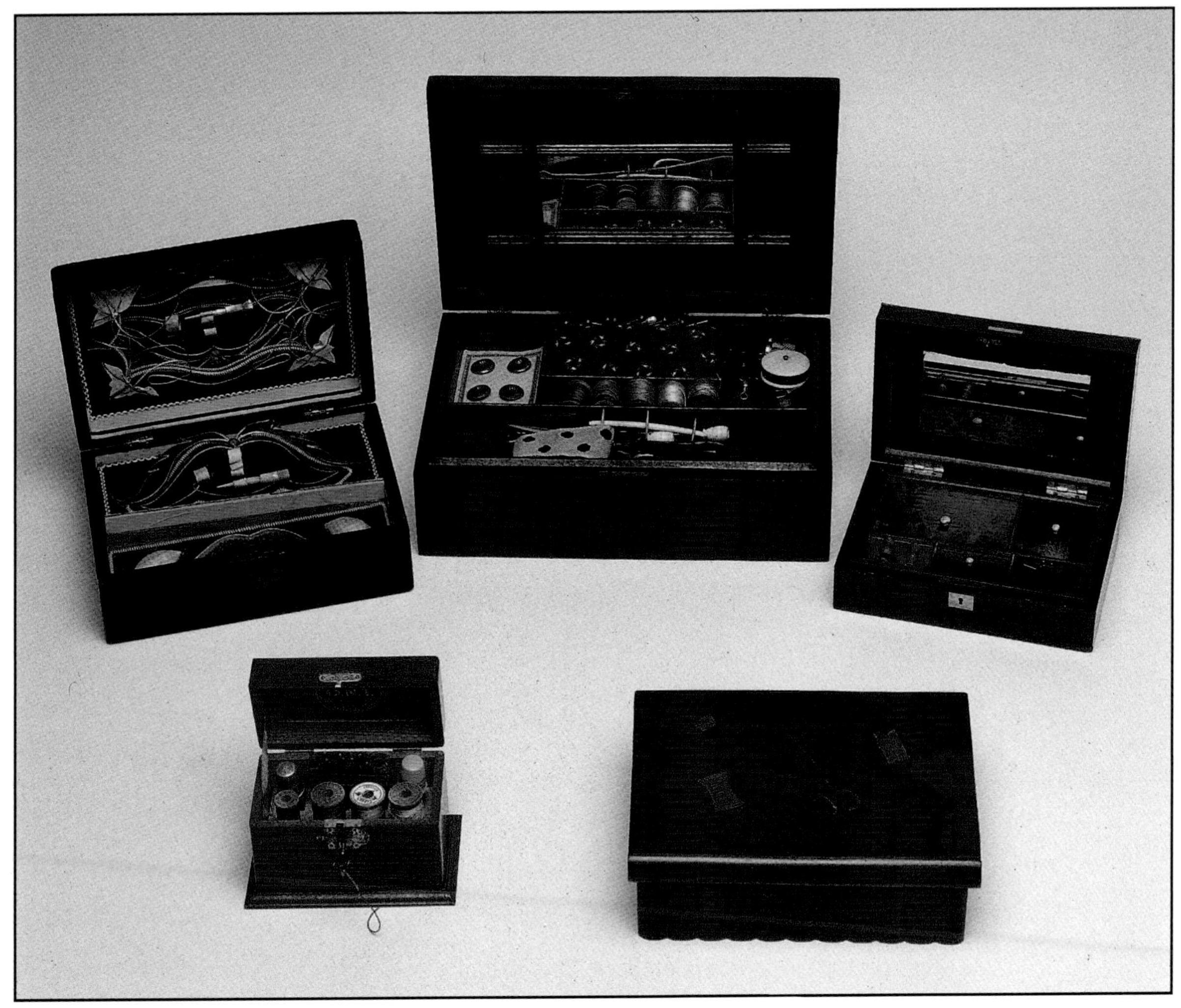

1st row:

1. England; black lacquer, transfer on the top, mirror decorated with silver leaves and cording, flocked inside, two small pincushions, a mother-of-pearl punch; c. 1875, $100.00.
2. USA; silver trim wood, mirror in top, pincushion and assorted sewing items; c.1900, $65.00.
3. England; wood, mirror, ivory knobs, mother-of-pearl key hole, two thread winders; c.1880, $120.00.

2nd row:

1. USA; Clark's ONT thread labeled oak box with lock and key, pincushion, thread, and thimbles; c. 1890, $125.00.
2. USA; walnut with maple inlay of a spool, scissors, needle holder, and thimble on top of box; c. 1910, $175.00.

USA; walnut sewing chest, manufactured by Charles Lane, New York, label on the back; china knobs, side spindles for thread, lift top drawer, pincushion, strawberry emery, brass eagle stick pin and pins and needles. The chest was an exhibit piece in the Miriam Tuska Quilt Exhibit at the Museum of the American Quilter's Society in Paducah, Kentucky, fall 1995; c.1880, $850.00.

1st row:

1. Scotland; ebony and satin wood; mosaic inlay; c. 1860, $300.00.
2. Massachusetts, USA; walnut with maple inlay of flowers, fan, stars, Masonic symbol lower center of lid, top of box has inlay initials "J.F.S.," bone knobs on section tops, wood section dividers covered with gold paper; c.1860, $500.00.

2nd row:

1. USA; Shaker, cherry, ivory finials and thread eyelets, pincushion mounted on top that lifts to reach thread chamber, two drawers, documented; c. 1880, $300.00.
2. Pennsylvania, USA; walnut and maple, same design as #1; c.1880, $175.00.

1st row:

1. – 4. England, France, or Spain; wooden boxes encrusted decorative combination of different shells, each one has a pincushion on top; souvenirs for export, often seaside resort and cities' names were added to the boxes. $60.00 – 85.00.
1., 3. Painted paper decal medallion in front of pincushion.

2nd row:

1. – 2. Same as top row except for shape; c. 1875, $55.00 – 75.00.
3. England; shell pincushion mounted on half shell, velvet lace trim, words engraved on side one "For A Dear Friend," on side two "Forget Me Not"; c. 1880, $55.00.

3rd row:

1. – 3. Pin safes of different shapes; c. 1875, $25.00 – 45.00.
4. – 5. Mollusk shell filled with pincushion, velvet; c. 1880, $25.00 each.
4. Trimmed with narrow, thin brass.
5. Trimmed with silk hanger.

Sears, Roebuck & Co., 1927

No. 8T7183
Fancy hanging double shell Pin Cushion. Sells easily for 25 cents.

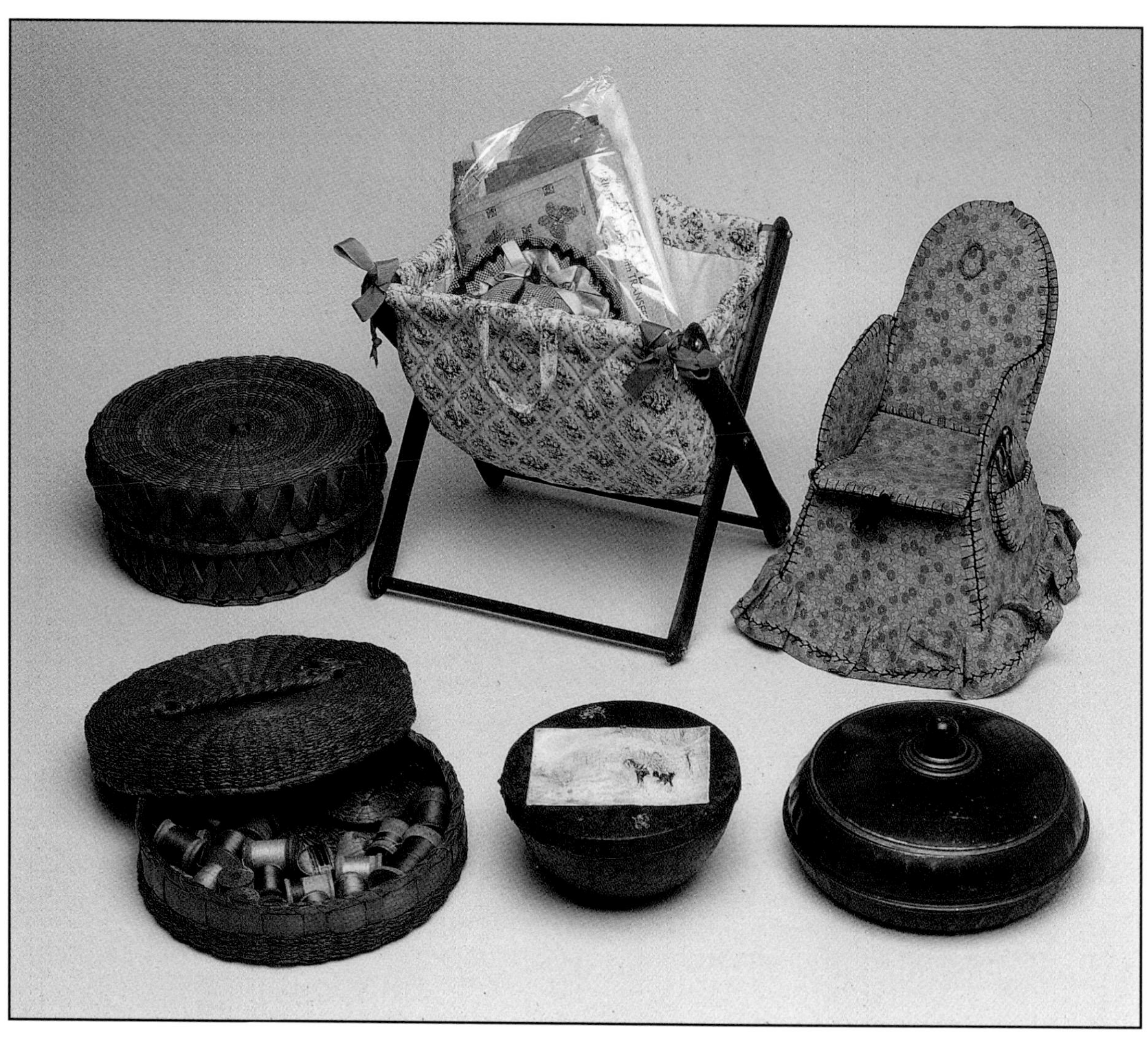

1st row:

1. USA; New England; Pemiquidic tribe, poplar splint basket; c. 1890, $100.00.
2. USA; sewing basket on walnut stand, cotton bag, a number of sewing items in bag; c. 1950, $25.00.
3. USA; Pennsylvania, chair sewing stand, the seat cover lifts for the storage area; c. 1940, $20.00.

2nd row:

1. USA; New England, Native American; poplar rim and ribs, woven sweet grass, covered sweet grass holder with tape measure, sweet grass needle and pin holder and spools of thread inside, braided sweet grass handle; c. 1890, $400.00.
2. England; leather with embossed celluloid scene, bone tools stored in slots on lid and larger pieces in bottom of the box; c.1880, $70.00.
3. USA; baked enamel sewing box, belongs to "Aunt Peggy"; c. 1940, $30.00.

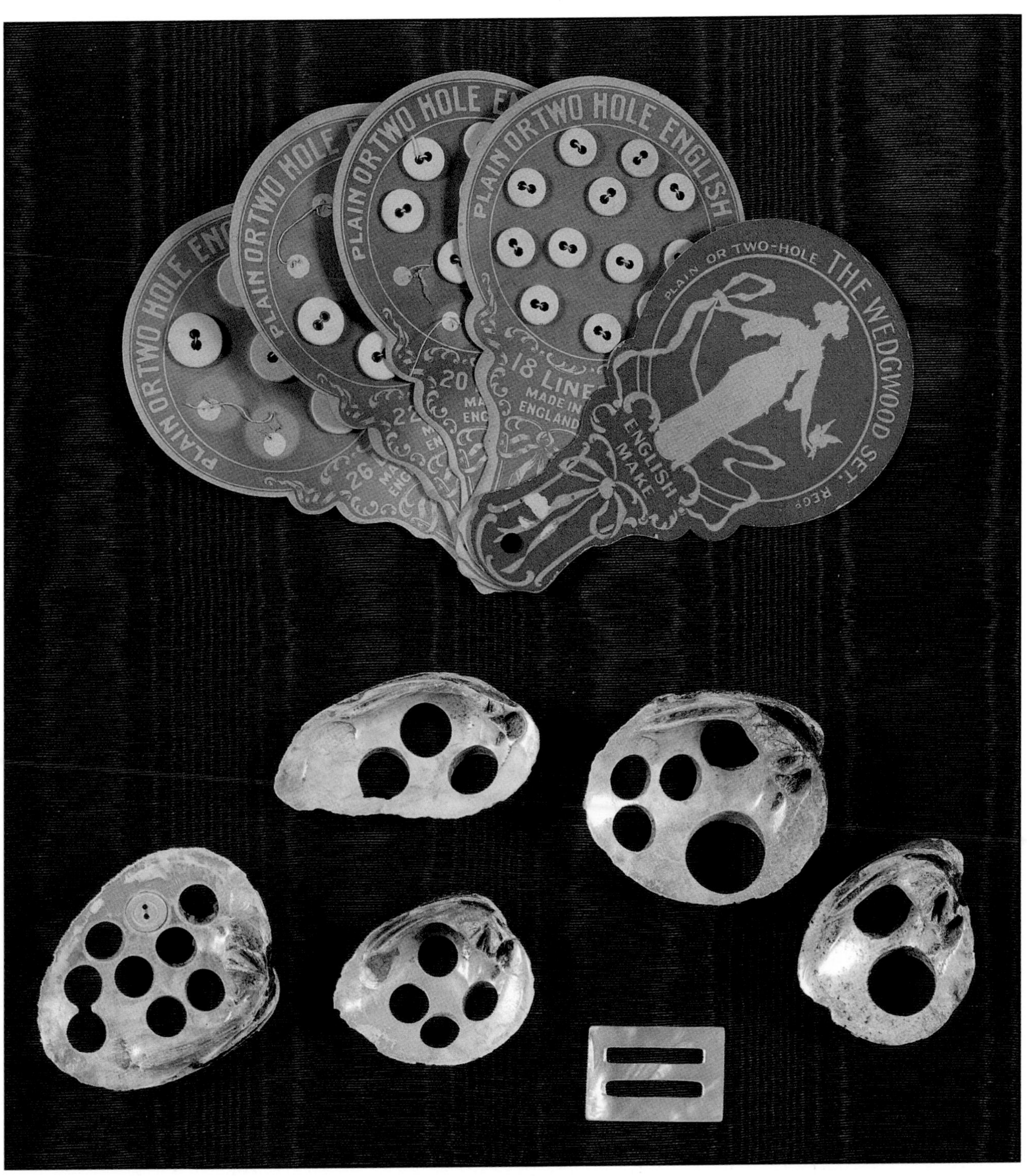

1. England; Wedgwood salesman's sampler buttons, the buttons are jasperware, $25.00.
2. Many kinds of shells have been used in producing sewing tools and buttons and buckles. These are Button Factory discards that were found along the Mississippi River. Salt water and fresh water shells were used for many different purposes throughout the world. Note the finished button resting in a cut-out of the first shell on left; c. 1900. $9.00 each.

Illinois quilting bee on the lawn; c. 1880, $35.00.

Stereograph of young girls quilting bee; c. 1880. Stereograph: a pair of stereoscopic pictures or picture composed of two superposed stereoscopic images that gives 3-D effect when viewed with a stereoscope. These were popular in late nineteenth century and early twentieth century.

Chapter Five

Scissors

Scissors have a long history. There is a drawing of a pair in a document from the twelfth century. They have been listed in inventory in some thirteenth century documents, and a pair can be seen in a stained glass window in Chartres, France. The early scissors were "spring" scissors," which were used by sheep shearers, farmers, groomsmen, housewives, and craftsmen. Some craftsmen's guilds used scissors in their coats of arms.

The basic design and construction of today's scissors originate in the sixteenth century when the spring scissors were gradually replaced. Beautiful scissors were exported throughout Europe from manufacturing towns in Italy, which were well known for quality of workmanship. There is reference to the Eastern influence that established strong centers of steel manufacturing in Italy and Spain during the Moorish occupation of these countries. Jewelers made beautiful scissors for the wealthy and ruling classes, where more utilitarian scissors, made of brass or iron, were used by the working class. Beginning in the Victorian period, it was common for the blades to be manufactured in Germany or England, and the handles to be added by manufacturers in a different country. An example of one of these combination pieces is shown on page 89. Scissors and other sewing items have been produced in miniature as charms, game pieces, and toys for dolls and young girls.

Germany; brass Art Nouveau dressmakers' scissors and sheath with a tulip-style motif, elegantly stylized handles; 9" c. 1890, $150.00. Exhibited in the Victorian Quilts Show, 1994, at the Museum of the American Quilter's Society, Paducah, Kentucky.

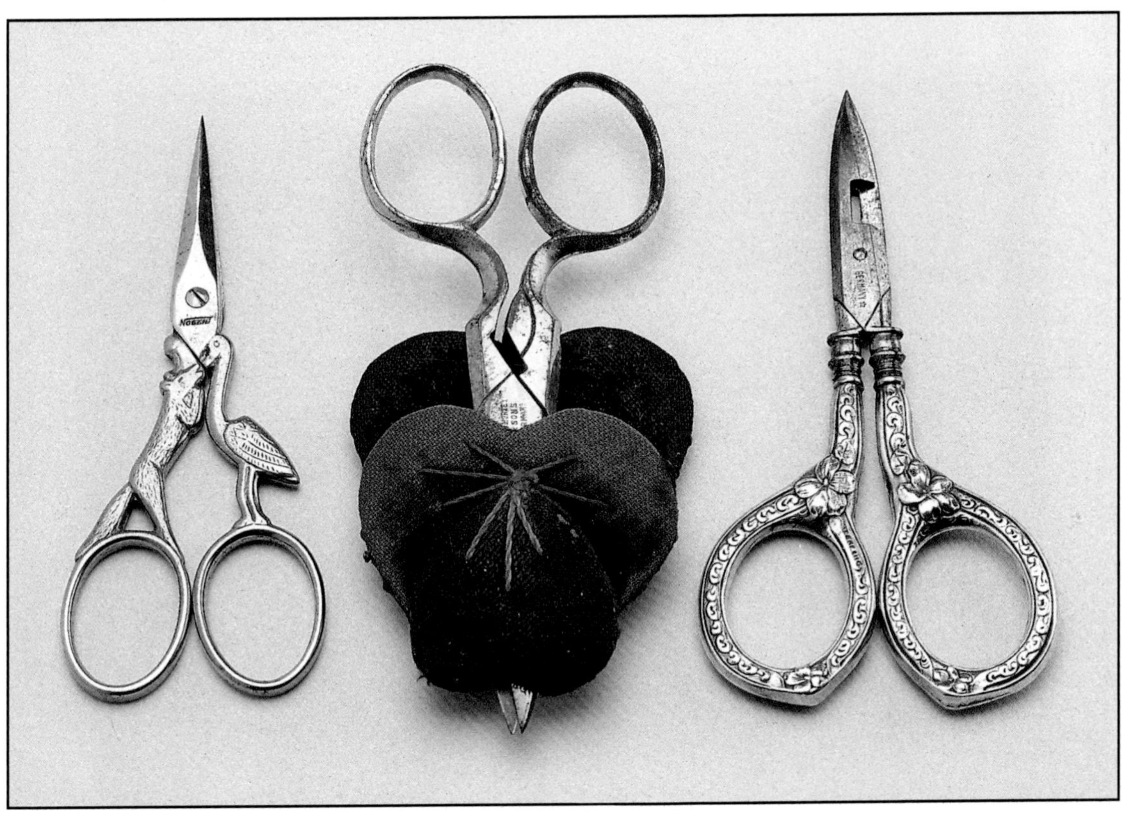

1. Germany; stainless steel, handles have a fox on the left and a stork on the right; c. 1920, $40.00.
2. Germany and USA; three heart-shape pin safes joined to make a sheath for German scissors; c. 1900, $20.00.
3. Germany and USA; buttonhole cutter and sterling handles; c. 1910, $70.00.

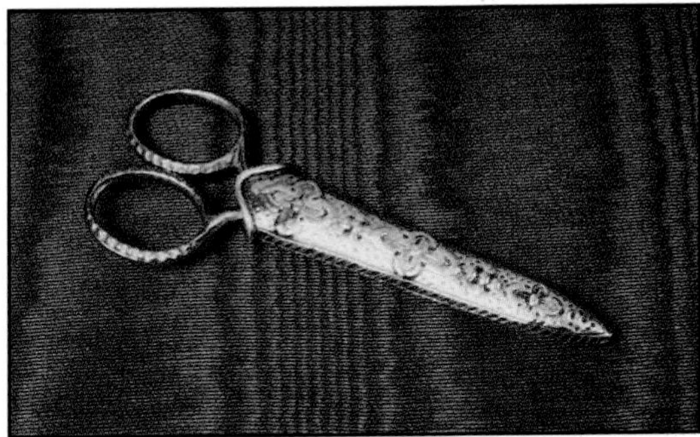

France; silver sheath with velvet lining, embossed design; c. 1860, $75.00.
Germany; cut steel scissors, stamped "made in Germany," bow knots on handles; 3½"; c. 1860, $85.00.

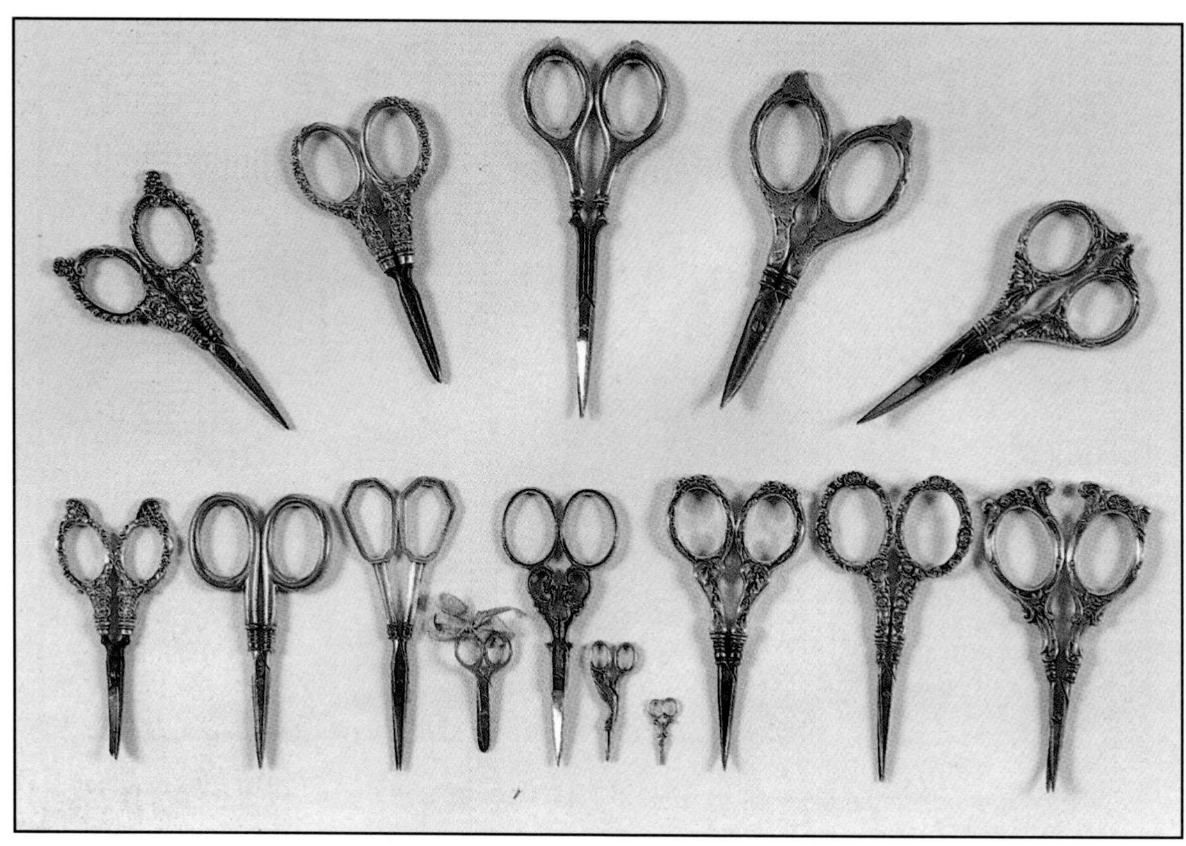

1st row:

1. – 5. Sterling handles; c. 1880, $40.00 – $60.00.
   2. Marked "RW&S Germany."

2nd row:

1., 2. USA; sterling; $35.00.
3. USA; sterling, marked "Pat. 1904"; 3½"; $45.00.
4. England; sterling, toy; 2¼"; c. 1900, $75.00.
5. Silver plate, "marked Hibbard, Spencer, Barlett & Co"; 3½"; c. 1910, $30.00.
6. England; sterling, stork reproduction miniature; 2"; 1990, $35.00.
7. England; sterling miniature; 1"; c. 1920, $70.00.
8. France; sterling, marked "France"; 3¾"; c. 1900, $55.00.
9. USA; sterling; c. 1915, $40.00.
10. England; sterling, hallmark "Birmingham, 1900"; $55.00.

The miniature pairs in positions 4, 6, and 7 are in working order, have sharp blades, and will cut; pairs 6 and 7 may have been considered charms.

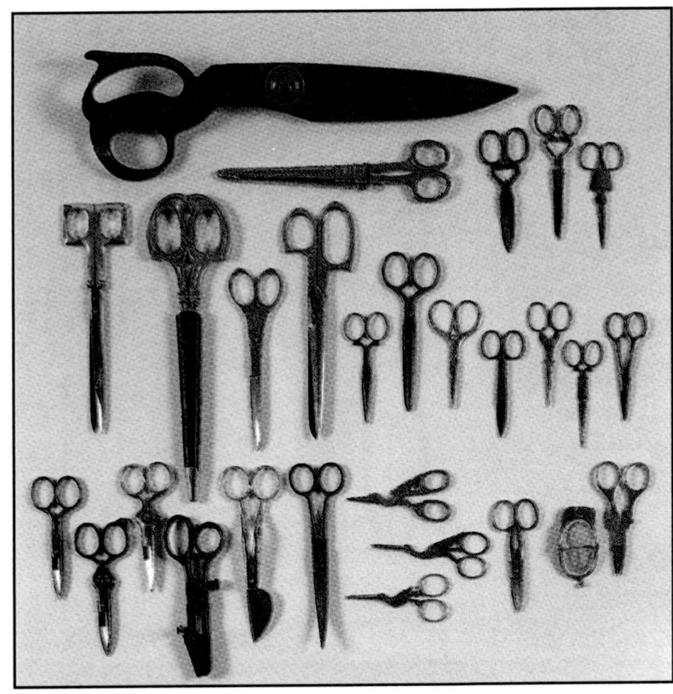

Right to left:
1st row:
1. USA; marked on brass joining "Pat. 1864 Newark, New Jersey," iron; 18"; $55.00.

2nd row:
1. Germany; steel, marked "Oremus Germany," butterfly handles; 3½"; c. 1890, $40.00.
2. Cut steel, snake handles, trademark "STERLING," "GEB.k. Germany"; c. 1890, $30.00.
3. England; gun-metal, snake handles; 4½"; c. 1900, $30.00.
4. Brass with brass sheath; 8"; c. 1910, $55.00.

3rd row:
1. England; steel, marked "James Dew Snap" Sheffield; 3½"; c. 1900, $20.00.
2. Cut steel, decorative handles; c. 1875, $15.00.
3. Prussia; cut steel, marked "SEARS" "PRUSSIA"; 3½"; c. 1900, $10.00.
4. England; cut steel, marked "Nogent"; 3½"; c. 1900, $7.50.
5. Polished steel, marked "USA"; 3½"; c. 1950, $5.00.
6. Steel, tradename "Lauterung"; 5½"; c. 1930, $7.50.
7. England; steel with flare handles, marked "BEST Sheffield"; 3½"; c. 1900, $15.00.
8. USA; polished steel, blades marked "Chicago Mail Order CO," "Eversham Forged Steel USA"; 8"; c. 1930, $10.00.
9. USA; steel, decorative handles; 6"; c. 1920, $15.00.
10. Germany; coin silver decorative handles; blades marked with a keg shape and "Germany," silver tip leather sheath; 10"; c. 1910, $55.00.
11. England, Germany, USA; sterling, steel blades marked "Von Cleef CO, Germany," handles marked with Simons Brothers CO shield, a lion's head, and "Cross, London"; 8"; c. 1915, $40.00.

4th row:
1. – 2. Spain; damascene-style gold and black finish on fold-up scissors, "Toledo" printed in gold on handle, soft leather snap purse, souvenir item; 3¾"; c. 1900, $12.00.
3. Germany; polished steel, embroidery; 3½"; c. 1930, $10.00.
4. – 6. Germany; stork, brass and steel; c. 1890–1920, $20.00–$35.00.
These style scissors were finished with gilt but it soon wore off with heavy use.
7. Germany; gun metal appliqué; c. 1880, $12.00.
8. USA; North Carolina, Fiskars, steel; c. 1980, $20.00–$40.00.
9. Gun metal, early button hole scissors with a guide bar; c. 1890, $12.00.
10. – 12. England, Germany, USA; polished buttonhole scissors; 4½"; c. 1910–1920, $18.00.

March 1, 1896.] THE YOUNG LADIES' JOURNAL. 207

SUPPLEMENTS CONTAINED IN THIS MONTH'S PART.

CUT-OUT PAPER PATTERN OF PELISSE FOR GIRL FROM FIVE TO SEVEN YEARS OF AGE.

For Illustration see Fashion Album; for Diagrams and Description see pages 10 and 11 of the Gigantic Supplement.

The Gigantic Supplement Comprises

A great variety of the latest Spring Fashions for Ladies and Children.

THE NEW ALBUM OF COLOURED PARIS FASHIONS for LADIES AND CHILDREN

Is described on page 11 of the Gigantic Supplement.

DESCRIPTION OF COLOURED FANCY-WORK SHEET.

SHOE-POCKET.

The foundation of the pocket is cream congress canvas, rather close in texture. It is shown in the full-size in the illustration. The piece of canvas for the front which forms the pocket is cut the depth shown, and 16 inches wide; this is arranged in two flat pleats, divided by a row of stitching. The embroidery is worked with blue flax thread, or with filoselle used four strands together, in buttonhole, satin, and cording-stitches. The entire edge is bound with blue ribbon ¾ inch wide; a bow of ribbon rather more than 1 inch wide ornaments the top. A small ring is sewn to the back of pocket behind the bow, by which to suspend it from the wall.

DESCRIPTION OF

Fashion Engravings,

Page 206.

No. 5.—HOME-DRESS.

This is a very simple and pretty dress, and is of lizard-green fine face cloth, trimmed round the foot with a band of moiré velvet the same shade; the bodice is new in style, it is of face cloth, trimmed with straps of narrow ribbon velvet, finished with silver buttons; the front side-pieces are of nut-brown velvet; the vest is of white cloth, trimmed on each side with small buttons, and crossed with straps of velvet; collet of moiré velvet, spreading over the shoulders, and finishing in square lappets on the bust; sleeves à gigot, ornamented with straps of velvet; collar of velvet, trimmed with passementerie; neckband of ribbon tied at the back.—Price of pattern of dress, made up, $1.25; flat, 50c. Bodice, made up, 60c.; flat, 25c.

No. 6.—WALKING-DRESS.

The dress is of brown striped camel-hair cloth, trimmed with bands of velvet arranged slantwise at the foot, and finished with gilt buttons; the bodice is slightly full, and has a vest of tan silk, it is ornamented at the waist with pointed tabs of velvet fastened with gilt buttons; godet sleeves trimmed with velvet; waistband of satin ribbon; cravat bow of chiffon. Hat of brown velvet, trimmed with shot ribbon, black ostrich tips, and clusters of lilac.—Price of pattern of dress, made up, $1 25; flat, 50c. Bodice, made up, 60c.; flat, 25c.

No. 7.—DRESS FOR GIRL FROM EIGHT TO TEN YEARS OF AGE.

The dress is of terra-cotta velveteen made quite plainly, with full sleeves à gigot; the pinafore of Nagpore silk entirely covers the skirt of dress and is edged with a full frill of cream lace, headed by a line of feather-stitching; the bodice is full, and is held in at the waist with a sash of striped ribbon tied at the back; the collet is rounded and spreads well over the shoulders, it is embroidered at the edge, and feather-stitched.—Price of pattern of pinafore, made up, 60c.; flat, 25c.

No. 1.—POCKET FOR SCISSORS.

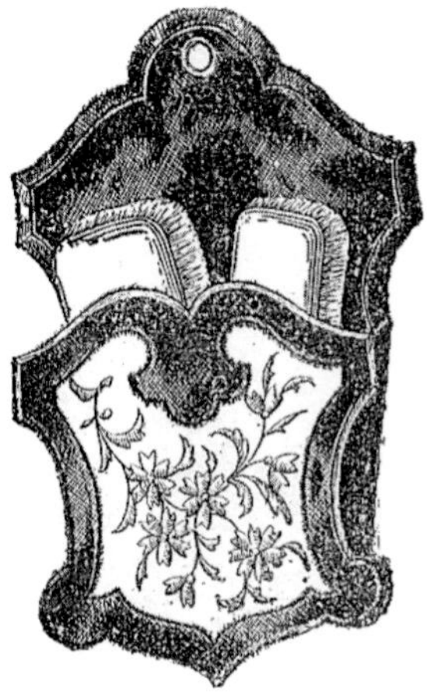

No. 2.—BRUSH POCKET.

No. 8.—WALKING-DRESS FOR GIRL FROM EIGHT TO TEN YEARS OF AGE.

The dress is of red and blue fancy foulé, trimmed round the foot with a band of red cloth stitched on each side; the bodice is tight-fitting, and has a pointed vest of cloth, edged on each side with ruchings of satin ribbon; full bishop sleeves gathered into narrow wristbands, and having full square epaulettes of cloth, edged with a narrow ruche. Hat of felt, trimmed with bows of wide ribbon velvet.—Price of pattern of dress, made up, 60c.; flat, 25c.

No. 9.—DRESS FOR GIRL FROM EIGHT TO TEN YEARS OF AGE.

The dress is of bluish-gray alpaca with a plain skirt, finished above the deep hem with a line of stitching; the bodice is tight-fitting and round-waisted, open in front to show a pleated vest of Indian silk, and turned back with square stiffened revers of velvet; three large buttons ornament each side of bodice; pointed waistband of velvet; sleeves à gigot of alpaca.—Price of pattern of dress, made up, 60c.; flat, 25c.

Orders and Remittances for Patterns or Subscriptions to THE YOUNG LADIES' JOURNAL, addressed to

J. GURNEY AND CO.,
No. 707, FULTON ST.,
BROOKLYN, NEW YORK.
P.O. BOX 3527, NEW YORK CITY,

will receive immediate attention. Canadian Stamps cannot be received in the United States. All payments for patterns must be made by Post-Office Order or United States stamps. 10c. extra should be remitted on all Canadian orders for cost of postage. Should replies be required, payment for postage of letter must be forwarded thus: 3c. for the U.S., 6c. for Canada.

DESCRIPTION OF

FANCY WORK.

No. 1.—POCKET FOR SCISSORS.

Who has not experienced the discomfort of losing one's scissors when cutting out and sewing? The little pocket shown in our illustration is intended to hang from the waist, so that the scissors may be put into it, and always be at hand when needed. It is composed of two pieces of cardboard; the piece for the back is cut 7 inches long and 3 inches across the widest part. It is pointed at each end, as shown in the illustration; the piece for the front is cut the same shape as the back as far as the widest part. It is cut a little wider towards the top so that it may set out from the back; both pieces of card are covered with brocade or fancy striped velvet; they are sewn together at the two sides, and the entire edge is finished with silk cord arranged in loops at the corners. A long loop of cord is sewn from each side by which to suspend it from the waistband, where it may be fixed by an ornamental safety-pin, or slipped over the band.

No. 2.—BRUSH-POCKET.

This is a useful pocket to hang in a dressing-room or hall. It is made on a foundation of very stout cardboard. The back measures 13 inches deep in the centre and 9 inches across; it is shaped as shown in the illustration, and is covered with burnt sienna-coloured plush, and lined at the back with sateen. A fine silk

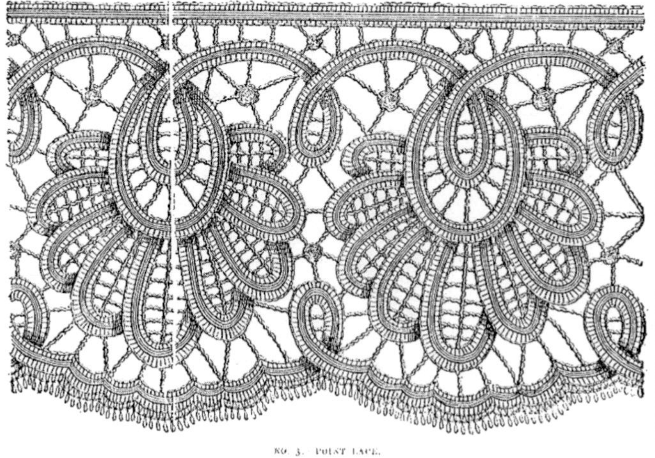

No. 3. POINT LACE.

The Young Ladies' Journal ad, March 1896.

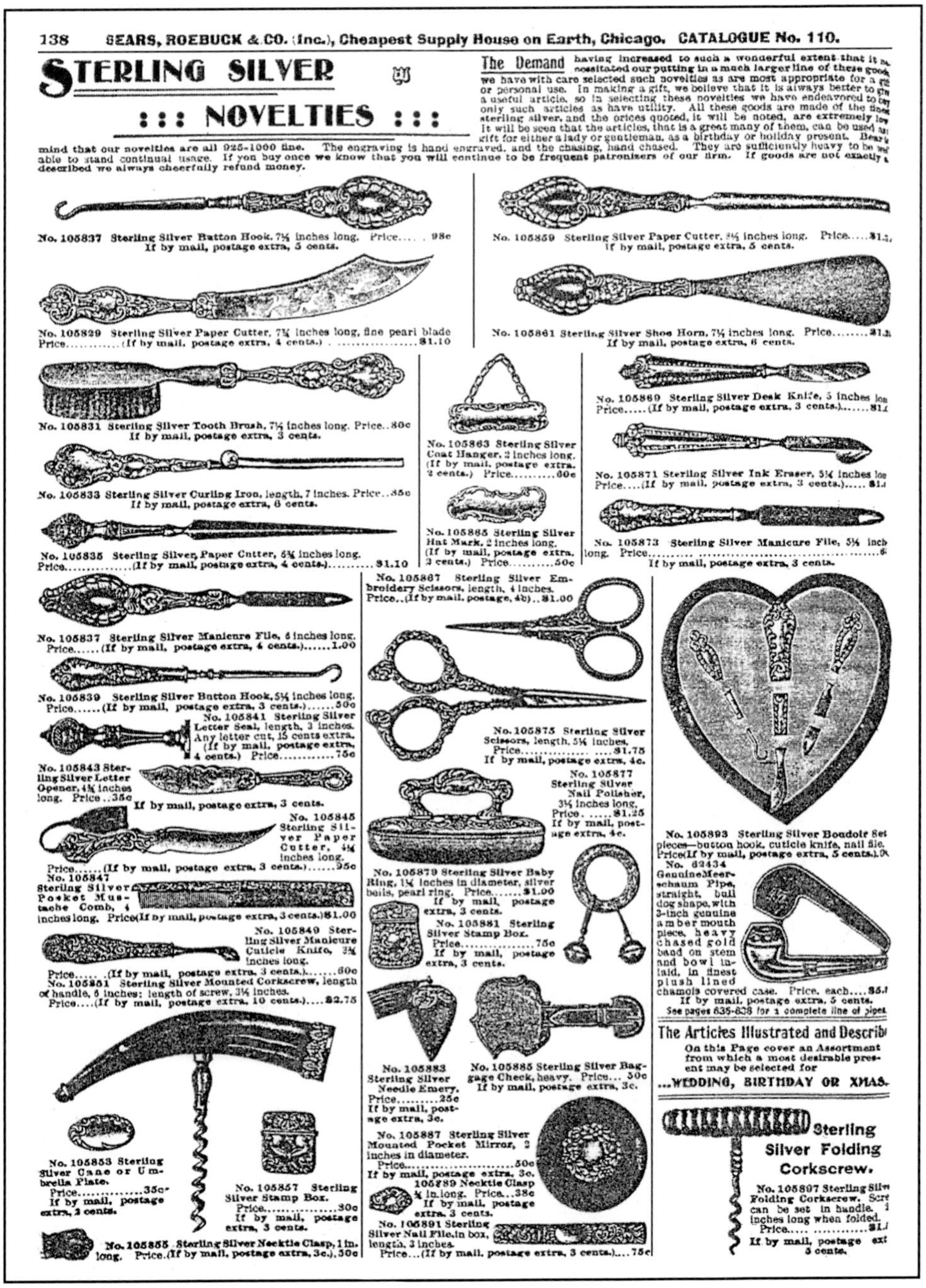

138 SEARS, ROEBUCK & CO. (Inc.), Cheapest Supply House on Earth, Chicago. CATALOGUE No. 110.

STERLING SILVER ::: NOVELTIES :::

The Demand having increased to such a wonderful extent that it necessitated our putting in a much larger line of these goods, we have with care selected such novelties as are most appropriate for a gift or personal use. In making a gift, we believe that it is always better to give a useful article, so in selecting these novelties we have endeavored to buy only such articles as have utility. All these goods are made of the finest sterling silver, and the prices quoted, it will be noted, are extremely low. It will be seen that the articles, that is a great many of them, can be used as a gift for either a lady or gentleman, as a birthday or holiday present. Bear in mind that our novelties are all 925-1000 fine. The engraving is hand engraved, and the chasing, hand chased. They are sufficiently heavy to be well able to stand continual usage. If you buy once we know that you will continue to be frequent patronizers of our firm. If goods are not exactly as described we always cheerfully refund money.

No. 105837 Sterling Silver Button Hook, 7¼ inches long. Price..... 98c
If by mail, postage extra, 5 cents.

No. 105859 Sterling Silver Paper Cutter, 8¼ inches long. Price.....$1.2
If by mail, postage extra, 5 cents.

No. 105829 Sterling Silver Paper Cutter, 7¾ inches long, fine pearl blade
Price...........(If by mail, postage extra, 4 cents.) $1.10

No. 105861 Sterling Silver Shoe Horn, 7¼ inches long. Price........$1.2
If by mail, postage extra, 6 cents.

No. 105831 Sterling Silver Tooth Brush, 7½ inches long. Price..80c
If by mail, postage extra, 3 cents.

No. 105863 Sterling Silver Coat Hanger, 2 inches long. (If by mail, postage extra, 2 cents.) Price..........60c

No. 105869 Sterling Silver Desk Knife, 5 inches lon
Price.....(If by mail, postage extra, 3 cents.)......$1.

No. 105833 Sterling Silver Curling Iron, length, 7 inches. Price..85c
If by mail, postage extra, 6 cents.

No. 105871 Sterling Silver Ink Eraser, 5¼ inches lon
Price....(If by mail, postage extra, 3 cents.)..... $1.

No. 105865 Sterling Silver Hat Mark, 2 inches long. (If by mail, postage extra, 3 cents.) Price..........50c

No. 105835 Sterling Silver, Paper Cutter, 5¾ inches long.
Price..............(If by mail, postage extra, 4 cents.).........$1.10

No. 105873 Sterling Silver Manicure File, 5¼ inch long. Price...$
If by mail, postage extra, 3 cents.

No. 105867 Sterling Silver Embroidery Scissors, length, 4 inches.
Price..(If by mail, postage, 4b)..$1.00

No. 105837 Sterling Silver Manicure File, 6 inches long.
Price......(If by mail, postage extra, 4 cents.)......1.00

No. 105839 Sterling Silver Button Hook, 5¼ inches long.
Price......(If by mail, postage extra, 3 cents.)......50c

No. 105841 Sterling Silver Letter Seal, length, 3 inches. Any letter cut, 15 cents extra. (If by mail, postage extra, 4 cents.) Price............75c

No. 105843 Sterling Silver Letter Opener, 4¾ inches long. Price..35c
If by mail, postage extra, 3 cents.

No. 105845 Sterling Silver Paper Cutter, 4¾ inches long.
Price......(If by mail, postage extra, 3 cents.)......95c

No. 105847 Sterling Silver Pocket Mustache Comb, 4 inches long. Price(If by mail, postage extra, 3 cents.)$1.00

No. 105849 Sterling Silver Manicure Cuticle Knife, 3¾ inches long.
Price...... .(If by mail, postage extra, 3 cents.).......60c

No. 105851 Sterling Silver Mounted Corkscrew, length of handle, 6 inches; length of screw, 3¼ inches.
Price....(If by mail, postage extra, 10 cents.)....$2.75

No. 105875 Sterling Silver Scissors, length, 5¼ inches.
Price............... ....$1.75
If by mail, postage extra, 4c.

No. 105877 Sterling Silver Nail Polisher, 3¼ inches long.
Price. $1.25
If by mail, postage extra, 4c.

No. 105879 Sterling Silver Baby Ring, 1¾ inches in diameter, silver bells, pearl ring. Price.......$1.00
If by mail, postage extra, 3 cents.

No. 105881 Sterling Silver Stamp Box.
Price..................75c
If by mail, postage extra, 3 cents.

No. 105893 Sterling Silver Boudoir Set pieces—button hook, cuticle knife, nail file.
Price(If by mail, postage extra, 5 cents.)1.0

No. 62434 Genuine Meerschaum Pipe, straight, bull dog shape, with 3-inch genuine amber mouth piece, heavy chased gold band on stem and bowl inlaid, in finest plush lined chamois covered case. Price, each....$5.
If by mail, postage extra, 5 cents.

See pages 635-638 for a complete line of pipes.

No. 105883 Sterling Silver Needle Emery.
Price..........25c
If by mail, postage extra, 3c.

No. 105885 Sterling Silver Baggage Check, heavy. Price... 50c
If by mail, postage extra, 3c.

No. 105887 Sterling Silver Mounted Pocket Mirror, 2 inches in diameter.
Price..........................50c
If by mail, postage extra, 3c.

105889 Necktie Clasp ¾ in. long. Price...38c
If by mail, postage extra, 3 cents.

No. 105891 Sterling Silver Nail File, in box, length, 3 inches.
Price...(If by mail, postage extra, 3 cents.).... 75c

The Articles Illustrated and Describ

On this Page cover an Assortment from which a most desirable present may be selected for

...WEDDING, BIRTHDAY OR XMAS.

No. 105853 Sterling Silver Cane or Umbrella Plate.
Price..............35c
If by mail, postage extra, 2 cents.

No. 105857 Sterling Silver Stamp Box.
Price................30c
If by mail, postage extra, 3 cents.

No. 105855 Sterling Silver Necktie Clasp, 1 in. long. Price.(If by mail, postage extra, 3c.).30c

Sterling Silver Folding Corkscrew.

No. 105897 Sterling Silv Folding Corkscrew. Scr can be set in handle. inches long when folded.
Price..... ....$1.
If by mail, postage ext 5 cents.

Sears, Roebuck & Co. catalog page, Fall 1900.

PATENT EUREKA SCISSORS

Have twenty times the cutting power of any ordinary scissors. Every pair guaranteed.

As Supplied to Royalty. Made of the very finest Steel.

PATENT EUREKA LADIES' SCISSORS, 4in. 1/8, 4½in. 1/9, 5in. 2/-, 5½in. 2/3, 6in. 2/6, 6½in. 2/8, 7in. 3/2, 8in. 4/4, per pair.
PATENT EUREKA TRIMMING SCISSORS, 6½in. 3/8, 7in. 4/-, 7½in., 4/8, 8in. 5/10 per pair.
PATENT EUREKA NAIL SCISSORS, 4in. 1/10 per pair.
PATENT EUREKA LAMP SCISSORS, 6½in. 3/8 per pair.
PATENT EUREKA FOLDING NAIL SCISSORS, 4/6 per pair.
Also Drapers' Scissors, 4½in. 2/3.

If not obtainable of your ironmonger, send P.O. and 3d. additional for postage to

MARTIN PULVERMANN & CO., 26, Minories, London, E.C.

The Young Ladies' Journal ad, March 1896.

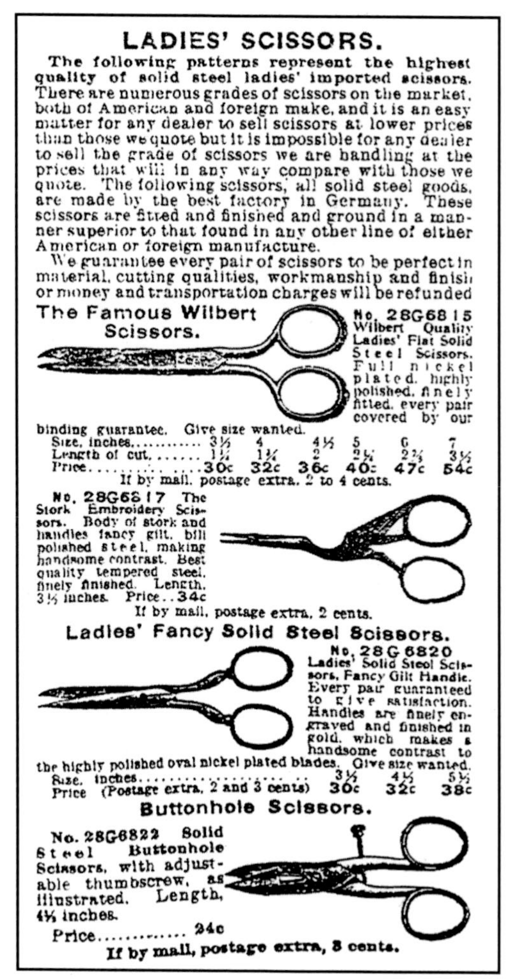

LADIES' SCISSORS.

The following patterns represent the highest quality of solid steel ladies' imported scissors. There are numerous grades of scissors on the market, both of American and foreign make, and it is an easy matter for any dealer to sell scissors at lower prices than those we quote but it is impossible for any dealer to sell the grade of scissors we are handling at the prices that will in any way compare with those we quote. The following scissors, all solid steel goods, are made by the best factory in Germany. These scissors are fitted and finished and ground in a manner superior to that found in any other line of either American or foreign manufacture.

We guarantee every pair of scissors to be perfect in material, cutting qualities, workmanship and finish or money and transportation charges will be refunded

The Famous Wilbert Scissors.

No. 28G6815 Wilbert Quality Ladies' Flat Solid Steel Scissors. Full nickel plated, highly polished, finely fitted, every pair covered by our binding guarantee. Give size wanted.

Size, inches	3½	4	4½	5	6	7
Length of cut	1½	1¾	2	2½	2¾	3½
Price	30c	32c	36c	40c	47c	54c

If by mail, postage extra, 2 to 4 cents.

No. 28G6817 The Stork Embroidery Scissors. Body of stork and handles fancy gilt, bill polished steel, making handsome contrast. Best quality tempered steel, finely finished. Length, 3½ inches. Price..34c

If by mail, postage extra, 2 cents.

Ladies' Fancy Solid Steel Scissors.

No. 28G6820 Ladies' Solid Steel Scissors, Fancy Gilt Handle. Every pair guaranteed to give satisfaction. Handles are finely engraved and finished in gold, which makes a handsome contrast to the highly polished oval nickel plated blades. Give size wanted.

Size, inches	3½	4½	5½
Price (Postage extra, 2 and 3 cents)	30c	32c	38c

Buttonhole Scissors.

No. 28G6822 Solid Steel Buttonhole Scissors, with adjustable thumbscrew, as illustrated. Length, 4½ inches.

Price............. 24c

If by mail, postage extra, 3 cents.

Sears, Roebuck & Co. ad, 1927.

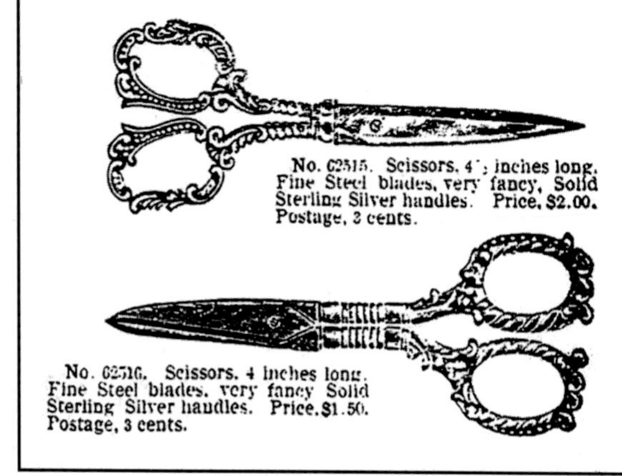

No. 62515. Scissors, 4½ inches long. Fine Steel blades, very fancy, Solid Sterling Silver handles. Price, $2.00. Postage, 3 cents.

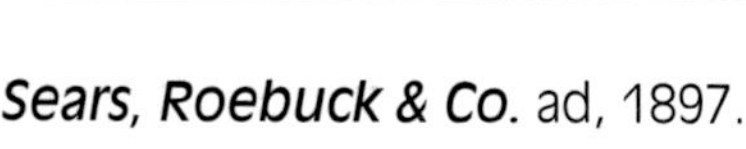

No. 62516. Scissors, 4 inches long. Fine Steel blades, very fancy, Solid Sterling Silver handles. Price, $1.50. Postage, 3 cents.

Sears, Roebuck & Co. ad, 1897.

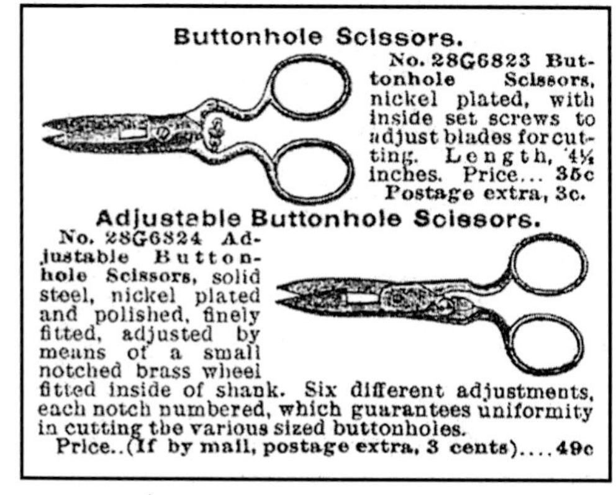

Buttonhole Scissors.

No. 28G6823 Buttonhole Scissors, nickel plated, with inside set screws to adjust blades for cutting. Length, 4½ inches. Price... 35c Postage extra, 3c.

Adjustable Buttonhole Scissors.

No. 28G6824 Adjustable Buttonhole Scissors, solid steel, nickel plated and polished, finely fitted, adjusted by means of a small notched brass wheel fitted inside of shank. Six different adjustments, each notch numbered, which guarantees uniformity in cutting the various sized buttonholes.

Price..(If by mail, postage extra, 3 cents)....49c

Sears, Roebuck & Co. ad, 1927.

Ladies Work
REVISED EDITION

Chapter Six

Tape Measures, Rulers, and Gauges

In 1855, the English Parliament authorized the standard yard, which was accepted by the United States in 1856. Prior to this date, it was common practice to provide your own measuring tool when purchasing fabric. Before the metric system was adopted in the early nineteenth century, the ell, which was the length from the shoulder to the elbow or the elbow to the fingertips, was a measure of length.

Early tapes were often encased in plain or sometimes very fancy cylinders with a slit long enough to allow the tape to move freely. They were attached to a finial that was turned by hand to roll the tape back into the canister. Sometimes there were small cranks to turn the tape. The tapes were made of silk or lightweight braid and were marked with black lines to indicate the measure. Occasionally, hand-painted flowers decorated the tapes. The casings were made of beautiful wood, ivory, mother-of-pearl, bone, filigree gold fill, silver, and brass.

Spring tapes were introduced in 1875. For attractive, less expensive tapes, celluloid was the ideal construction material. The molded, figural celluloid tapes of late 1800 through 1940 are greatly sought after by collectors. Many of these were manufactured in Germany and Japan. Tape measures have been a successful souvenir item as well as an advertising tool for businesses, politicians, resorts, and other forms of tourism. With the exception of celluloid, the materials used to make tape measure casings have not changed.

Tape measures, both the very old and newer varieties, are a source of great delight for collectors, due to their availability and diversity.

England; Victorian lady's tape, floral enamel, brass over copper rim, spring tape, good condition; c. 1890, $75.00.

USA; Native American, celluloid, "Niagra Falls" on back, souvenir; c. 1900, $250.00.

1. Germany; celluloid ship, yard measure; c. 1900, $75.00.
2. Scotland; tartan ware, McGregor tartan, wood painted black, finial rewinds, cotton yard-long tape; c. 1875, $200.00.

1st row:

1. Japan; celluloid pig, spring tape, marked "Occupied Japan"; c. 1947, $45.00.
2. China; silver-plate reproduction, made in Shanghai for export, hand crank unrolls and rolls up tape; 1¾" x 1½"; c. 1990, $35.00.
3. Celluloid, painted pig, spring tape; c. 1915, $75.00.
4. USA, Chimney Rock, NC, souvenir; c. 1920, $20.00.
5. USA; prosthesis ad, spring tape; c. 1930, $10.00.
6. USA; painted china head, spring tape; c. 1915, $65.00.
7. Germany; brass owl face with glass eyes, spring tape; c. 1900, $45.00.

(Prices continued on page 99.)

(Prices Continued from page 98.)

2nd row:

1. Asia; pierced vegetable ivory barrel-shape, ivory finial for winding and unwinding cloth tape, ivory pull; 1¾"; c. 1880, $55.00.
2. Germany; Terrier Stephen graph, spring tape, marked "Germany West Zone"; c. 1947, $165.00.
3. England; man smoking a cigarette tape pull, celluloid; c. 1900, $190.00.
4. Germany; celluloid basket of fruit, spring tape; c. 1915, $70.00.
5. Japan; celluloid hen and chicks, spring tape; c. 1920, $75.00.
6. Japan; celluloid terrier and puppy, spring tape; c. 1915, $85.00.

3rd row:

1. Canada; souvenir, "London, Canada" on one side, a mirror on the other side, decorative blue celluloid band, metal, spring tape; c. 1910, $45.00.
2. Asia; carved vegetable ivory, tape and thimble holder, tape with ivory pull and ivory finial; c. 1880, $150.00.
3. Asia; pierced ivory and vegetable ivory tape and needle holder; c. 1890, $65.00.
4. Asia; column style, pierced ivory tape holder, stanhope mounted on center section, shows a country mansion; c. 1880, $85.00.
5. Asia; acorn; vegetable ivory with carving of palm leaves, ivory pull and finial; 2"; c. 1880, $65.00.
6. Tunbridge Wells, England; mosaic ware tape measure with ivory pull, natural color woods; 1½"; c. 1860, $125.00.

4th row:

1. Asia; vegetable ivory tape holder with vegetable ivory pull and finial, carved; 2½"; c. 1875, $75.00.
2. China; mother-of-pearl top, ivory holder, red silk tape, part of a work box; c. 1875, $65.00.
3. Asia; ivory acorn with blue silk tape; c. 1875, $175.00.
4. England; man's hat, Isle of Man (decal); celluloid spring tape; 1½"; c. 1900, $70.00.
5. Germany; Spanish American War helmet-style rolled tin; brass eagle, braid, and finial; 1½" x 2¼"; c.1890, $225.00.
6. Germany; brass clock, arms move clockwise when tape is pulled; face and cover celluloid; c. 1890, $95.00.

5th row:

1. England; brass thimble shape with man sewing, tape measure, man is the finial; c. 1870, $225.00.
2. England; silver, blue silk tape; 1"; c. 1860, $80.00.
3. England; wood with brass tape crank, braid tape; ½" x 1"; c. 1890, $55.00.
4. England; gold fill, dome top, crank for rewinding tape, silk tape; ½" x 1"; c. 1860, $95.00.
5. England; pig, nickel plate worn off, fine brush stroke on body; brass tail is crank; c. 1890, $45.00.
6. England; silver plate over brass, silver tape pull; c. 1890, $95.00.
7. USA; sterling with Greek key design, Webster CO, spring tape; c. 1900, $75.00.
8. England; brass with crank for tape; c. 1880, $50.00.

1st row:

1. Battle Creek, MI, USA; three pieces "Instruction Book for the Kellogg French Tailor System MME KELLOGG, Inventor and Patentee," patent 1880, sleeve and dart rule, folding square and bias rule, the system awarded diplomas when the course of instruction was completed; MMe. Kellogg's System won gold, silver, and bronze medals at the Cincinnati Exposition 1882, 1883, she also held the patent for a double adjustable tracing wheel; $55.00.
2. USA; The Ladies Work Basket Ruler, wood, on the back "compliments of Bigelow Dry Good Store, VanWert, Ohio; maker Wesco H Jewel Co, Seneca, Falls, NY," 6"; c. 1930, $15.00.
3. USA; sterling, folding four-part ruler, Webster CO, monogram "P H"; 12"; c. 1900, $150.00.

2nd row: Hem gauges

1. – 5. USA, sterling.
   1. "Pat. Oct 2 '94," decorative slide; 3"; $250.00.
2. – 4. Webster, CO, slide; 3"; c. 1910–1920, $75.00 – $95.00.
5. S Kirk and Son, monogram "S," 4"; $110.00.

3rd row:

1. USA; "Tuscaloid" ruler (celluloid) ad, The Meek Company, Cosocton, Ohio, folding, 12"; c. 1915, $25.00.
2. USA; Brass hem gauge, "patented June 27, 1871; Feb 3, 1874," measure: ¼", ½", ¾"; $30.00.
3. USA; "Measure Up To the Goals" games, three years and up, produced by The Michael Jordan Foundation; distributed by Target Stores; $25.00.

Chapter Seven

Darners

With few exceptions, darners are no longer in use as household tools. They are most certainly collectible, the most common example being the egg-shaped darner with a handle. There are many variations of the wooden darner: natural, painted black, marbleized, ebony, and the German parquet (pieces of different woods glued together and then cut to shape, creating a checkerboard look). The handles of these darners were not only plain, but also made of decorative silver work, Russian enamel over brass (see page 103), and silver with a stone cap. There are wooden darners in the ball foot form and, as produced by the Boye Company, a dome-topped darner with a flat bottom (page 104).

The most popular darners are the blown and molded glass examples that are also called whimsies. These darners come in a single color, such as the foot form; shadings of one color to another, such as the "peach blow"; and the multi-colors, such as the "end of day." Another example of a glass darner was the white "nesting egg," a small handy item. There were a number of factories in the United States and Europe that produced these glass darners or whimsies.

"DARN IT! The History and Romance of Darners" by Wayne Muller is an interesting and worthwhile addition to any collector's library.

1. New England, USA; ball frosted with "Home Sweet Home" and pictures of a cabin, stars, new moon, and leaf garland, letters and pictorial cut into a steel die, die filled with powdered glass or "frit" which was picked up with a glove of molten glass; dark blue-green, open end, 7½"; $250.00.
2. USA; small ball on short handle, clear glass with small bubbles, free blown, closed ground pontil, solid handle with slight yellow color; 3"; $35.00.

1st row:

1. England; hallmark, London, 1920, sterling handle, ebony egg; 4"; $65.00.
2. Russian enamel handle, ebony egg; 6" c. 1900, $100.00.
3. USA; painted egg, sterling handle, amethyst set in end of handle, maker's mark "F&B"; 6"; c. 1890, $200.00.
4. Ebony egg and sterling handle; 6"; c. 1910, $65.00.
5. – 8. Marbleized paint over wood; 6"; c. 1900, $35.00.

Center: Glove darners
Top: Marbleized paint over wood; 2 sizes; $10.00.
Center. Sterling; two sizes; $60.00.
Lower. Painted wood, two sizes; c. 1920, $15.00.

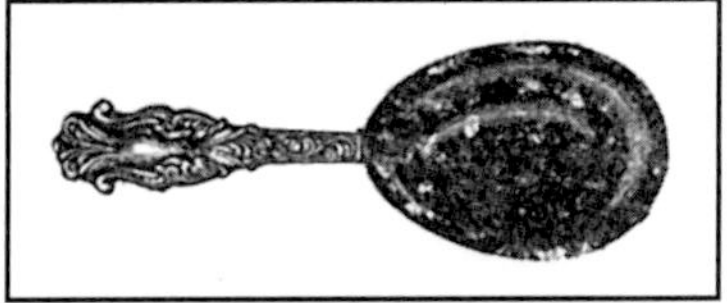

Sears, Roebuck & Co., 1900

1. – 3., 5. Salem, Massachusetts, USA; foot form, mold brown, tradename "KRISTL," dark green, amber, light green, blue; c. 1940, $75.00.
4. Cambridge, Massachusetts; USA; New England Glass Works, peach blow, shades to a white handle, single layer, free blown, glossy finish; 6"; c. 1900, $200.00.
6. Czechoslovakia; etched on handle, light blue, egg shape; c. 1915, $70.00.
7. USA; amber, ball on glove darner handle, free blown, one layer; c. 1940, $85.00.
8. USA; chicken egg (nest egg), free blown, closed; $10.00.

The nest eggs were available and easy to clean for uses other than encouraging hens and their egg production.

Clockwise starting at top center:

1. Germany; wood stickware, turned handle, egg shape; 6"; $75.00.
2. Wood, mushroom shape; 4½"; $25.00.
3. Wood, child's size, stained; $7.00.
4. Wood, bat shape; $5.00.
5. Germany; wood, mushroom shape, checkerboard, painted handle; 4½"; $35.00.
6. Germany; wood, mushroom, burnt-wood German lettering on top of mushroom; 4½"; $25.00.
7. Wood glove darner; 4"; $10.00.
8. Wood; foot form, "Pat. Nov 1907"; 5½"; $15.00.
9. Germany; stamped on top, mushroom checkerboard, red dyed and natural wood; 5¼"; $35.00.
10. Germany; wood stickware mushroom; 5"; $50.00.
11. Plastic, sock and glove, marked "Hungerford Darn-Aid"; 6"; $15.00.

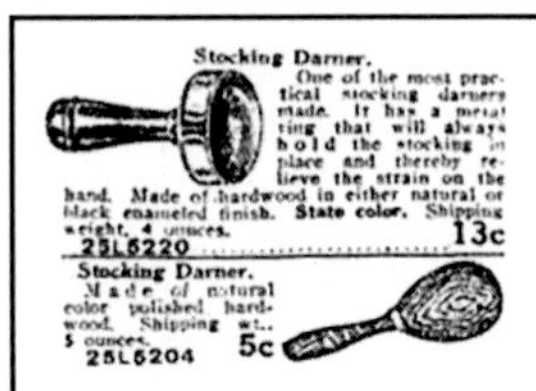

Stocking Darner. One of the most practical stocking darners made. It has a metal ring that will always hold the stocking in place and thereby relieve the strain on the hand. Made of hardwood in either natural or black enameled finish. **State color.** Shipping weight, 4 ounces.
25L6220 13c

Stocking Darner. Made of natural color polished hardwood. Shipping wt., 5 ounces.
25L6204 5c

Sears, Roebuck & Co., 1923

Center:

Top: England; yew wood; egg shape; 2½"; c. 1990, $40.00.

Center: USA; maple, darning knob style, made by Boye Needle Co., Chicago, patent 1936, 1¼"; $35.00.

Lower: USA; wood double glove darner; c. 1920, $15.00.

HOOKED RUGS
with
"Susan Burr"
Extra fine Nainsook Quality
Embroidery Edging
Dust Proof
ORIGINAL QUALITY

Chapter Eight

Lacemaking Tools and Accessories

Lace has been described as "the fine flower of the decorative arts." It is an open-work fabric constructed of intertwining, looping, and knotting threads with specific tools. Lace is not a practical, utilitarian fabric, rather, it is made for the adornment of clothing and table and household linens. It was stylish for men in the seventeenth and eighteenth centuries to wear lace collars. Handmade lace, as an industry, began to decline in the late nineteenth century as a result of the Industrial Revolution.

Bobbin and needlepoint laces, in contrast with the laces produced by crochet, knitting, macrame, and tatting, are considered the true laces since they produce a fabric. See page 107 for an example of bobbin lace and a view of a work in progress. Needlepoint lace is made by drawing a design on the back of a coarse canvas, and then creating the needlework. When the needlework is complete, the designs are removed from the backing and sewed onto netting.

Lacemaking tools, bobbins, pillows, and needle kits are available as long as the collector is patient. Tools for crochet, knitting, and tatting are readily available. The containers that were made for these tools may take some time to locate. Beautiful wooden lacemaking boxes, made in Asia for export, can be found, but many have been dismantled and the tools sold individually,

Stereograph: c. 1880 lacemaking class and general sewing class for young girls.

Asia; ivory, clamp and silk winder, these two pieces probably came out of a lacemaker's box that was dismantled; c. 1865, $65.00 – 85.00.

England; bobbin lace pillow covered with floral print fabric, ten wooden bobbins, four slender, two with beads, six heavy plain bobbins, lace in progress, 11½" x 11½"; c. 1900. $300.00.
The pillow has a roller in the center, the pattern is placed on the roller, and pins in the pattern are used as a guide for the thread that has been wound on the bobbins. The lengths of lace in progress drop in a catch bag behind the roller. Lace bobbins have been made of different materials, although largely of wood and bone. Some are plain, while others have very complex decorative work. English bobbins are largely from the East Midlands.

Handmade lace handkerchief with Irish linen center, center 4" x 4", overall 12" x 13"; c. 1870, $30.00.

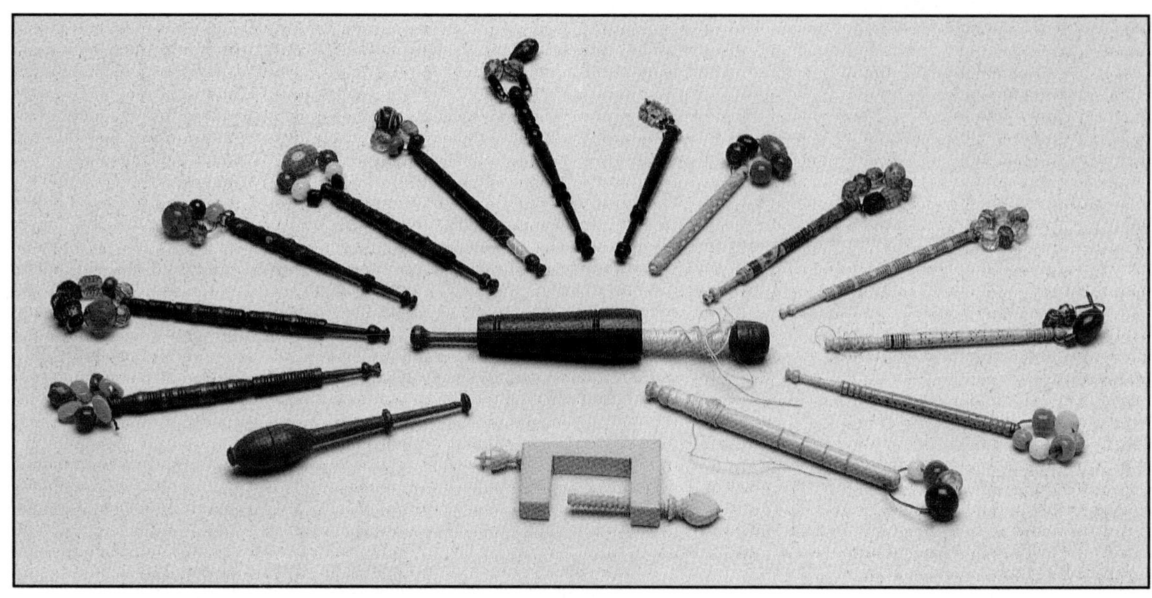

Lacemaking bobbins
Center:
1. Germany; wood, thread protector; 5¼"; c. 1940, $15.00.
2. Asia; ivory clamp, originally a piece of a lacemaking box and had a thread winder on top opposite finial; c. 1880, $75.00.

Clockwise starting bottom left: England; #2 – 14 glass beads.
1. Wood, plain; c. 1920, $5.00.
2. – 5. Wood, decorated with pewter inlay.
6., 7. Ebony, turned.
8. Wood with intricate small bead work.
9. Bone, small carved indentations.
10. Bone decorated with wire work and paint.
11. Bone decorated with a series of painted circles.
12. Bone, "Emma" punches and painted.
13. Bone, two straight lines of punches.
14. Bone, plain, round top.
2. – 14. C. 1880, $45.00 – 75.00.

Lacemaking bobbins were designed for size and weight and often personalized and decorated.

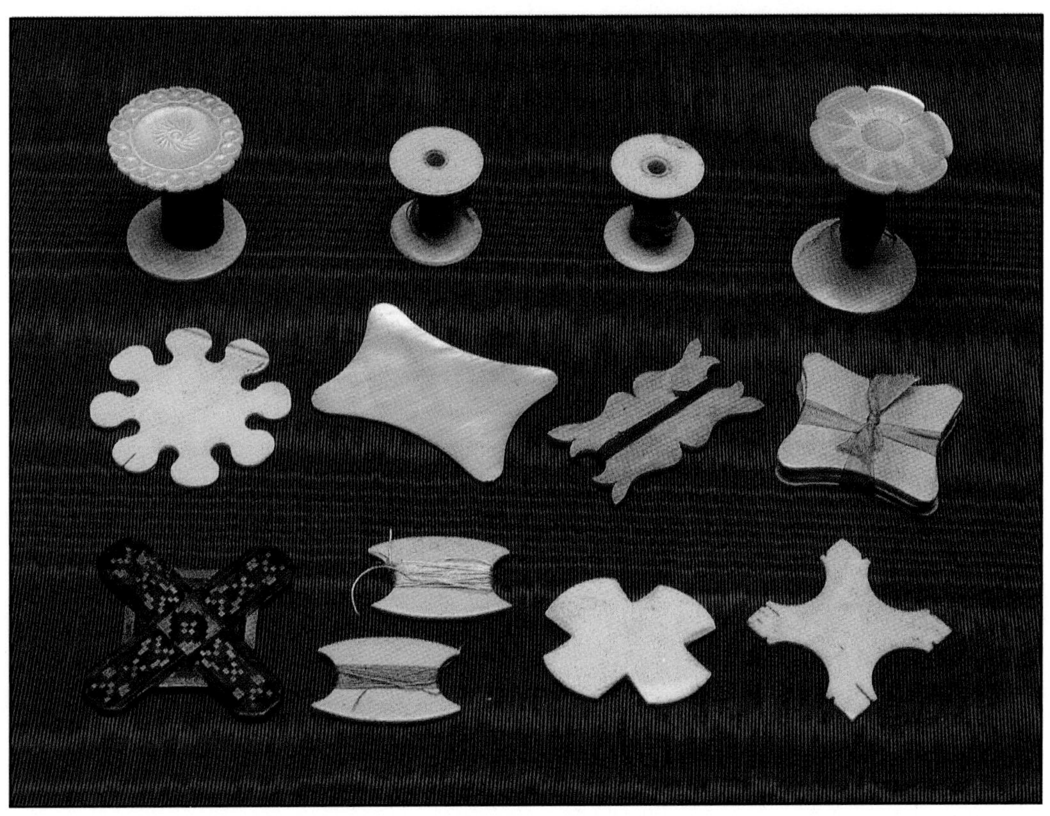

1st row:
- 1. – 4. England; reels.
- 1., 4. Mother-of-pearl carved tops, metal shaft, ivory base, parts will unscrew from each other; c. 1875, $60.00.
- 2., 3. Ivory reels, also unscrew; c. 1880, $40.00.

2nd row: Silk winders.
- 1., 3. England; ivory; c. 1880, $50.00 – 75.00.
- 2. England; mother-of-pearl; c. 1900, $45.00.
- 4. England; set of six, ivory, silk ribbon; c. 1880, $50.00.

3rd row: Silk winders.
- 1. England; tunbridge mosaic pattern winder; c. 1875, $225.00.
- 2., 3, 5. England; ivory, work box pieces; c. 1875, $30.00 – 40.00.
- 4. USA; bone, hand carved; c. 1900, $45.00.

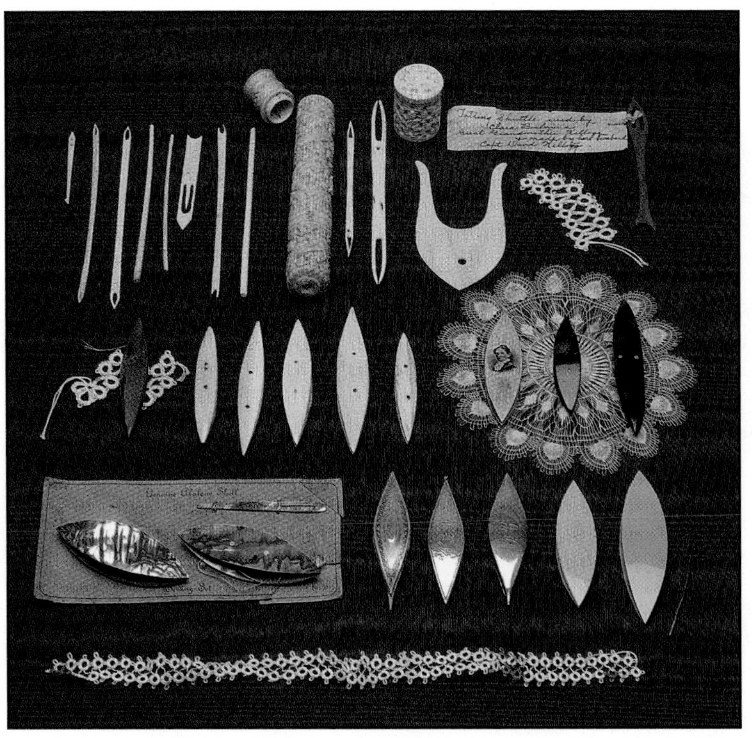

1st row:

1. – 9. China; ivory net needles and three netting mesh (#4, 5, 8), ornately carved case and top; this is a complete set; c. 1880, $100.00.
10., 11. China; bone netting needles; c. 1880, $20.00 each.
12. Asia; carved ivory thread holder, a piece from a lacemaking work box; c. 1890, $30.00.
13. Lucet; ivory; used for making braid and chains; c. 1875, $150.00.
14. USA; sample of tatting; c. 1920, $10.00.
15. USA; New England, netting needle, handmade, wood; note attached: "Tatting shuttle used by Clara Bulmer's Great Grandmother Kellog & made by Captain David Kellog." The similarity of design of #6 and #15 is the reason for calling it a netting needle rather than a tatting shuttle sometimes called netting shuttle; c. 1860, $75.00.

2nd row:

1. England; ivory, red stained, on a sample of tatting; c. 1890, $55.00.
2. – 6. USA; bone tatting shuttle; c. 1900, $25.00.
7. Kentucky, USA; beautiful lace medallion; c. 1890, $25.00.
8. – 10. USA; celluloid.
   8. Lydia Pinkham, Ad; c. 1915, $75.00.
   9. – 10. Fake tortoise; c. 1910, $10.00 – 30.00.

3rd row:

1. USA; two abalone tatting shuttles and a bodkin on original manufacturer's display; c. 1910, $125.00.
2. – 4. USA; sterling.
   2., 3. Webster Company; c. 1920, $75.00 – 85.00.
   4. Nussbaum & Hunold, Providence, RI; c. 1930, $60.00.
5., 6. USA; two celluloid tatting shuttles; c. 1920, $7.50 each.

4th row:

USA; sample of tatting lace; c. 1920, $15.00.

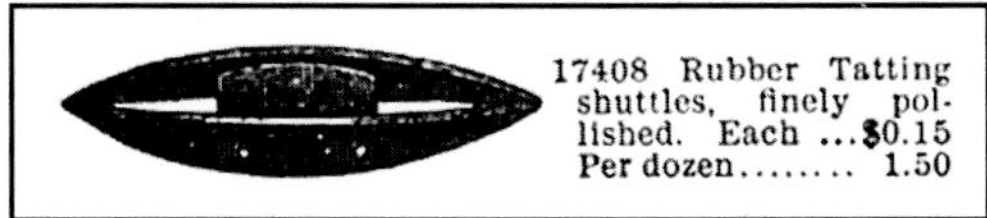

Montgomery Ward Co. catalog, fall/winter 1894 – 95

1st row:
1. USA; wood crochet hook; 13"; c. 1940, $7.50.

2nd row:
1., 2. USA; crochet coaster and a dresser scarf; c. 1920, $3.00 – 5.00.
3. England; leather case, agate handle with crochet hook, originally there three interchangeable hooks in the set; c. 1875, $150.00.
4. USA; bone crochet hook; c. 1910, $5.00.

3rd row: Crochet hooks
1. Umbrella-style needle case, three bone crochet hooks, one punch with metal tip cover, the case is painted wood, natural varnish tip and handle, nickel over copper fittings; c. 1910, $85.00.
2., 3. USA; sterling handle with very fine hook; c. 1900, $30.00 – 40.00.
4, 8., 9. England and USA; metal protective cylinder or shield for hooks, each has slide to retrieve hook; c. 1870, $35.00 – 50.00.
    4. Decorative painted cylinder.
    8., 9. Combination steel and decorative brass.
5., 6. USA; two hand-carved bone hooks; c. 1920, $10.00.
7. USA; bone handle with etched "stork scissors" image, stamped on back "Diadem" Pat. Aug 17, 1915; $15.00.
10. USA; "Susan Bates," plastic; c. 1950, $1.00.
11., 12. England; Milward Co., steel; c.1910, $5.00 each.
13.–15. USA; Boye Co., steel; c. 1930, $3.00 each.

Box, top:

1. Bone bodkin.
2. – 6, 8. Bone, different size crochet hooks.
7. Bone, punch.
9. Bone, long very fine crochet hook.
10. Bone, thimble.

Box. Purple velvet pincushion; 3".

Piece lay out: (from the box)

1st row:

1. Metal, homemade hair pin lace tool.
2. – 4. Metal, three commercial hair pins used to make hair pin lace.

2nd row:

1. – 2. Celluloid tatting shuttles, white and black.
3. – 6. Finishing needles with heavy thread.
7. – 8. Two punches, 7 metal, 8 bone.
9. – 13. Metal Boye crochet hooks and container.
14. Florida souvenir, ivory.
15., 16. Hand whittled, wood crochet hooks.

This box came out of a central Kentucky home, and is made of leather and has a silk lining; c. 1890–1910, $95.00.

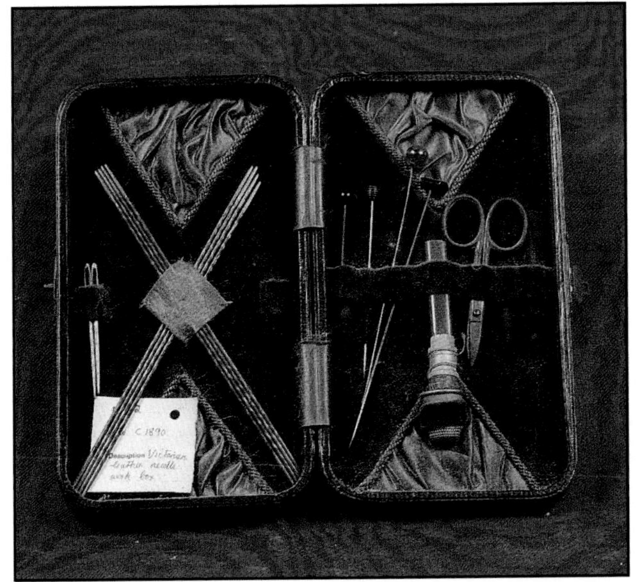

England; black leather work box, satin and silk lining, left side has two tapestry needles, four pair gold tip knitting needles with blue and gold design, right side has four long glass head pins, gun metal scissors, unusual needle, thread, and thimble holder; c. 1890, $100.00 – 125.00.

1st row:

1. England; Mauchline Scottish transfer ware, wood with scene of "Old Village Shanldin," contains four different size knitting needles and a finishing crochet hook; c. 1865, $120.00.
2. Italy; carved wood column, four different size knitting needles; 10"; c. 1870, $75.00.
3. England; "London," brass bell shape knitting needle sizer; c. 1890, $25.00.
4. USA; tracing wheel, wood and steel with spoke wheel; c. 1940, $10.00.
5. USA; wood, double crochet hook, handmade; 5"; c. 1915, $5.00.
6. USA; steel seam ripper; c. 1910, $7.50.
7. USA; latch hook with hand carved handle; c. 1940, $4.00.
8. USA; latch hook with wood handle; c. 1950, $5.00.
9., 10. USA; information folder "The Making of Hooked Rugs with Susan Burr Hooked Rug Machine" manufactured by The Holley Associates, Torrington, Conn," the folder has historical information and directions with photographs, the machine is maple with brass fittings and looper, steel needle, trademark on lower brass fitting; c. 1920, $35.00.

March 1, 1896.] THE YOUNG LADIES' JOURNAL. 171

DESCRIPTION OF

FASHION ENGRAVINGS,

Page 170.

No. 1.—MORNING-DRESS.

This is a very simple little dress, but at the same time is stylish; it is of bright greenish-blue Zuper cloth, with a plain skirt, trimmed with a narrow strapping; the bodice is tight-fitting, and is pointed back and front; it is trimmed with narrow strappings, extending from the shoulders to below the waist in front, and shorter at the sides; each strap terminates under a gilt button; the sleeves à gigot are very full in the upper parts, but are buttoned from elbow to wrist, and finished with narrow strappings.—Price of pattern of dress, made up, $1.25; flat, 50c. Bodice, made up, 60c.; flat, 25c.

No. 2.—HOME-DRESS FOR MATRON.

The dress is of tan-colour poplin, trimmed round the foot with a band of green bengaline, headed by a narrow fancy gimp, combining the two colours; the bodice is tight-fitting, and has a yoke and vest of green bengaline; the basque is of poplin, rather deep, and very full at the back; it is edged with a scalloped band of bengaline; sleeves à gigot, buttoned at the wrist; collar of poplin, with tabs of bengaline falling over.—Price of pattern of dress, made up, $1.25; flat, 50c. Bodice, trimmed, 60c.; flat, 25c.

No. 3.—EVENING-DRESS.

The dress is of white satin, with a very full skirt; the front width is embroidered at the foot with gold thread and cord, and arranged in pleats at the sides; the bodice remains open, and has loose fronts embroidered with gold and lined with yellow satin; the vest is tight-fitting, and trimmed across with six flat bows of yellow ribbon velvet; short puffed sleeves; pleating of satin round the neck, edged with ribbon velvet.—Price of pattern of dress, made up, $1.25; flat, 50c. Bodice, made up, 60c.; flat, 25c.

No. 4.—DRESS FOR GIRL FROM EIGHT TO TEN YEARS OF AGE.

The dress is of gray foulé, with a full skirt, trimmed round the edge with a band of poppy-red velvet; the bodice is turned back with double square revers, and shows a tight-fitting vest; both revers and vest are trimmed with velvet; sleeves à gigot, with square stiffened epaulettes.—Price of pattern of dress, made up, 60c.; flat, 25c.

Orders and Remittances for Patterns or Subscriptions to THE YOUNG LADIES' JOURNAL addressed to
J. GURNEY AND CO.,
No. 707, FULTON ST.
BROOKLYN, NEW YORK,
P.O. BOX 3527,
NEW YORK CITY,
will receive immediate attention. Canadian Stamps cannot be received in the United States. All payments for patterns must be made by Post-Office Order or United States stamps. 10c. extra should be remitted on all Canadian orders for cost of postage. Should replies be required, payment for postage of letter must be forwarded thus: 3c. for the U.S., 6c. for Canada.

THERE is a world of pathos in the remark of a poor woman coming from a wretched garret in an inland town, and seeing the ocean for the first time. Gazing steadily at it, in perfect silence, for some minutes, she sighed and said, slowly, "Well, I am glad for once in my life to see something of which there is enough."

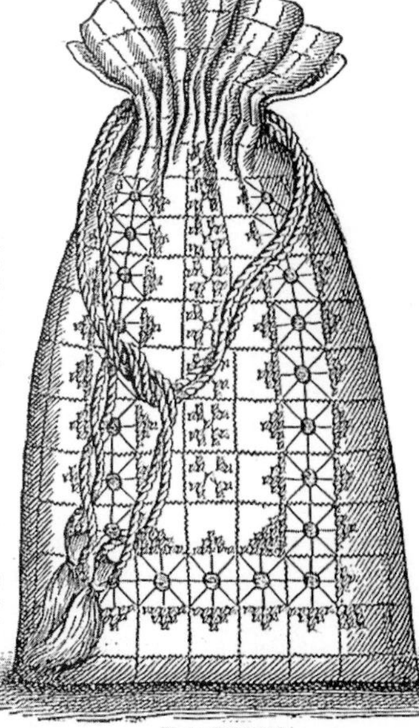

NO. 1.—WORK-BAG.

NO. 2.—DESIGN FOR NO. 1.

DESCRIPTION OF

FANCY WORK.

NOS. 1 AND 2.—WORK-BAG.

This is a most useful bag for keeping crochet in, or any white work requiring to be kept very clean, as being made of washing material it can be washed frequently. The foundation of the bag is fine linen glass cloth, woven with a blue line in squares. It is cut 16 inches wide and 15 inches long; both sides are ornamented with the design shown in No. 2, worked with blue ingrain cotton of two shades, the darker shade being used for the cross-stitch, and the lighter for the spun-stitches. The linen is sewn together at the bottom and up the side to within 6½ inches of edge, where it is turned down 3¼ inches to form a frill and a running slide through which cord, finished by tassels, or ribbon with a bow on each end, should be run. Of course the size of the bag must be regulated to a certain extent by the size of the square woven in the linen, as it is not always possible to obtain it with the exact size squares shown; but the work on a little larger scale will look equally well.

THE HOME.

ECONOMICAL COOKERY.

Lentil Purée.—1 pint red lentils, 1 onion, ½ head celery, 1 oz butter, pepper, salt, 2 quarts water.—Cost, 6d. Wash the lentils well in water, put them in a stewpan with the butter, onion peeled and sliced, and celery cut in pieces; stand the saucepan over the fire for 5 minutes, add the water, and simmer for 1 hour; pass it through a sieve, put back in the saucepan with pepper and salt to taste, give one boil, and serve.

Baked Mackerel.—2 mackerel, 1 dessertspoonful chopped herbs and onions, 1 dessertspoonful chopped parsley, ½ oz breadcrumbs, pepper, salt, 2 oz dripping.—Cost, 9d. Wash the mackerel, dry them, and put them on a board; cut off the heads, slit open the fish, and remove the backbone, lay the fish open flat on a tin, skin underneath; chop the parsley, onion, and herbs very finely, add the breadcrumbs, and season rather highly, put it on the fish, lay the other mackerel on top, pour the dripping melted over the fish, put a cover on the tin, and bake ½ hour.

Irish Stew.—2 lb potatoes, 2 lb middle of the neck of mutton, 1 lb onion, pepper, and salt. —Cost, 1s. 6d. Wash the potatoes well, peel and cut them in slices; peel the onions, and cut them in slices also; rub the mutton with a damp cloth, and cut in small pieces; put it in a saucepan with the potatoes and onions on top, then another layer of meat, potatoes, and onions, sprinkling salt and pepper between each layer; pour in ½ pint cold water, let the stew boil, then skim it, and stew gently for 1½ hour, taking care it does not burn; turn on to a dish, and serve very hot.

Meat Fritters.—Slices of cold meat, batter. Cut the meat in squares, and dip each piece in a rather thick batter, having previously sprinkled it with pepper and salt; let them stand a little while, then again dip in the batter, and fry in boiling lard till of a golden brown; pile on a dish, and garnish with parsley.

Date Rolly Pudding.—½ lb suet crust, 1 lb dates.—Cost, 8d. Make a rather rich suet crust, and roll it out in an oblong ½ inch thick; stone the dates, slightly chop them, and lay them on the paste; roll it up, pinch the ends together, tie in a floured cloth, and boil for 1½ hour; serve with sweet or custard sauce.

The Young Ladies' Journal, March 1896.

DESCRIPTION OF FANCY WORK,

Continued.

No. 3.—TRIMMING: CROCHET.

This very handsome design may be used for a variety of purposes; worked with cream, écru, or light brown cotton it will make a lovely mantle or bracket drape. With white or cream cotton it is suitable for a collarette. To make it fit round the throat a ribbon should be run through the row of trebles just below the scallops, the patterns only being joined together as far as the beginning of the deep scallops; these scallops spread out over the shoulders.

Commence in the centre of rosette of the top part with 11 chain, join round.

1st Round: 10 doubles under the chain draw through 1st double.

2nd Round: * 16 chain, work down the chain with 1 double into the 2nd and each of 13 following stitches, 1 chain, turn, work 1 double into each stitch, 1 chain, turn, work 1 double into each stitch, pass over 4 stitches, 1 double into the next, repeat from * 7 times more, draw through first of first 16 chain, then break off the cotton and fasten neatly at the back of the work. For the picot row, work 1 double into the fifth stitch from the top of bar, 5 chain, 1 double into the point, 4 chain, one double into the first, * 1 treble into the centre line of doubles, 5 chain, 1 double into the first, repeat from * twice more, 1 double into next corner, 5 chain, pass over 4 stitches, 1 double into the next, 6 chain, 1 double into the second, 1 chain, repeat from the beginning of the row 7 times more.

For the straight perpendicular line in the centre of point, make a chain of 73 stitches.

1st Row: Pass over 4 stitches, 1 double into the next, to form a picot, 4 chain, pass over next 4 stitches of foundation chain, * 1 cross treble worked as follows: turn the cotton twice over the hook, insert it in next stitch, work off 1 loop, pass over 3 stitches, 1 treble into the next, work off the rest of loops one at a time, 3 chain, 1 treble into centre of cross, 1 chain, pass over 1 stitch, repeat from * 8 times more, 3 chain, pass over 3 stitches, 1 treble into the next, 2 chain, pass over 2 stitches, 1 half treble into the next, 3 chain, 1 single into end stitch.

2nd Row: 1 chain, 3 doubles into end stitch, 1 double into each stitch until you reach the stitch but one before the picot, then work 1 double into a picot at end of arm of rosette, 5 chain, 1 single into next picot, pass over 1 stitch past the picot, work 1 double into each stitch, draw through first double.

3rd Row: * 9 chain, pass over 1 chain, 1 double into each of 8 stitches, 1 chain to turn, 1 double into each stitch, 1 chain, 1 double into each double, pass over 2 doubles of foundation, 1 double into each of 7 next stitches, repeat from * 7 times more, working 10 instead of 9 chain each time after the 1st. When you have worked the 7th repeat, work 1 double into each of 3 doubles, then work the row of picots round the * as follows: *, 6 chain, 1 double into the second, repeat from * twice more, 2 chain, 1 double into picot of rosette, 6 chain, 1 double into the second, 2 chain, 1 double into the next picot, repeat from * 7 times more with the exception that 3 picots only are worked between 4 lower arms of rosette, 5 between the others. As will be seen from the illustration some of the picots are turned up and some down, and at the top more stitches are worked between some picots than others; this must be regulated by the worker as some persons work chain so much tighter than others, and the number of stitches must be arranged so that the work lies flat; work down the other side of perpendicular bar like the first side, draw through first stitch of row.

4th Row: Work 1 single into each of 4 of first 8 chain, *, 11 chain, 1 single into the 6th, 1 treble into end of first line of doubles, 2 trebles separated by a picot of 5 chain into next bar, 1 picot, 1 treble into same bar, 1 picot, 1 double into end of next bar, 6 chain, 1 double into centre stitch of third line of doubles, 9 chain, 1 double into fifth, 2 chain, 1 double into side of next bar of doubles, then repeat from * 7 times more, 2 chain, work 1 single into the row of picots worked round rosette, break off the cotton and fasten it securely at the back of work; the second side is worked as described for the first, care being taken to fasten the ends of cotton off securely and neatly.

No. 3.—TRIMMING: CROCHET.

The 5th Row begins the scalloped edge, which is worked round each point, 1 double into centre of 3 picots at left-hand side of rosette, 6 chain, 1 double into the second, 6 chain, 1 double into the second, 1 double into end picot of second arm from the bottom of rosette, 6 chain, 1 double into second picot of first bar of doubles of point, 6 chain, 1 double into the second, 1 chain, 1 double into next picot, 11 chain, 1 double into sixth, 3 chain, 1 double into picot on next bar of doubles, 6 chain, 1 double into the second, 2 chain, 1 double into the next picot; all the picots are worked as already described, 3 turned inward between each of the bars of doubles, and 1 turned out between the picots at end of bar. For the 3 lower scallops allow 3 chain between each picot.

6th Row: 3 trebles each separated by 2 chain into the second picot of fifth row, 5 chain, 1 double into next picot, * 5 trebles each separated by 1 chain into centre of 5 chain before next picot, 4 chain, 1 double into next picot, 4 chain, repeat from * 5 times more, then enlarge the 3 lower scallops by working 6 double trebles separated by 2 chain into the same picot, and work 5 instead of 4 chain before and after the double worked into the single picot. Work up the second side as described for first.

7th Row: 2 trebles separated by a picot between each of the three first trebles, 4 doubles under chain between scallops, 2 chain, * 2 trebles under next chain; keep the top of each treble on the hook, and draw through both together; 5 chain, 1 double into the second, 1 chain, repeat from * 3 times more, but do not work a picot after last repeat of trebles, work instead 2 chain, 4 doubles between scallops. All except the 3 lower scallops are worked in this way; for the 3 lower scallops work 3 trebles between each of the trebles of last row, keep the top loop of each on the hook, and draw through all together; for the picots, 6 chain, 1 double into the second, 1 chain, work 6 clusters of trebles on each scallop and 6 picots; work 7 doubles between each of the 3 lower scallops. When the second pattern has been worked, the rosettes must be joined by a line of picots, which are attached by doubles worked into the last row of picots worked round rosette.

For the heading:

1st Row: 1 treble into the scallop between the centre and right hand bar of a rosette, * 6 chain, 1 treble between 2 next picots, repeat from * twice more, 12 chain, 1 double into the seventh, * 5 chain, 1 double into the first, repeat from the last * 7 times more, joining the third picot by 1 single to the row of picots round the rosette, form the picots into a loop by working 1 double into stitch before the first picot, 8 chain, 1 double treble into the line of picots joining the rosettes.

2nd Row: 1 treble into a stitch, 2 chain, pass over 2 stitches, and repeat.

3rd Row: 1 double into a stitch, 4 chain, pass over 6 stitches, 5 trebles each separated by 2 chain into next, 4 chain, pass over 6 stitches, and repeat.

4th Row: 1 double into double between scallops, 5 chain, * 2 trebles worked as described under next chain, 6 chain, 1 double into second, 1 chain, repeat from * twice more, 2 trebles between next trebles, 5 chain, repeat from the beginning of the row.

THE PROPRIETORS OF THE YOUNG LADIES' JOURNAL beg respectfully to inform their numerous subscribers that they have made arrangements with Messrs. Wakeford Bros., Art Needlework Emporium, of 102 to 106, King's Road, Sloane Square, London, to supply them with every requisite for Art Needlework to the minutest particular, at strictly wholesale prices. Wakeford Bros. publish an interesting Novelty Catalogue, which is sent to any part of the world post free. Knitting Yarns are kept at 1s. 11d., 2s. 6d., 2s. 11d., 3s. 1d., and 3s. 7d. per pound. Wheeling Yarns, for Shooting, and Golf Hosiery at 1s. 11½d., 2s. 4½d., 2s. 6d., and 2s. 11d. N.B.—To save time, subscribers are requested to send direct to Messrs. Wakeford Brothers.

PARIS FASHIONS.

DEAR EVELYN,

You say you will be more interested in the simple dresses of Mlle. L——'s wedding than in those of the young Countess de C——, so I will now tell you of some of them. The bride herself was in white satin, for in spite of many attempts at innovations, satin seems to be the one and unique tissue for bridal dresses, whether rich or simple. It is certainly very becoming with its soft, sheeny folds, and can either be made quite plain or elaborately trimmed, at pleasure. The only trimming on the dress consisted in delicate trails of orange buds and blossoms placed on each seam of the front width, and similar trails en bretelles upon the plain, tight-fitting bodice, finished a few inches from the waist by chou rosettes of satin. Drooping sleeves full to the elbow and tight to the wrist, with a lace frilling falling over the hand, headed with a bracelet of

The Young Ladies' Journal, March 1896.

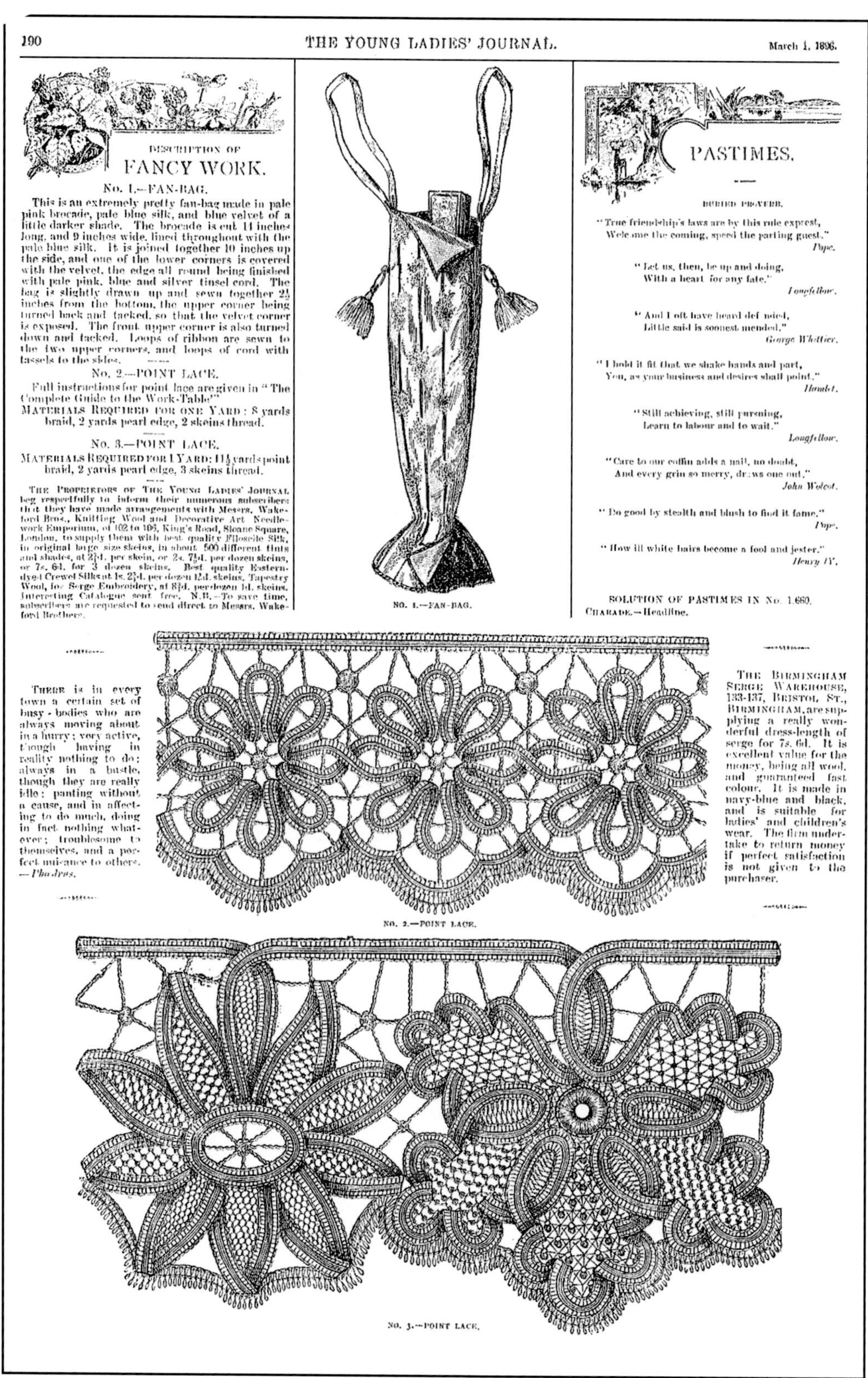

DESCRIPTION OF

FANCY WORK.

No. 1.—FAN-BAG.

This is an extremely pretty fan-bag made in pale pink brocade, pale blue silk, and blue velvet of a little darker shade. The brocade is cut 14 inches long, and 9 inches wide, lined throughout with the pale blue silk. It is joined together 10 inches up the side, and one of the lower corners is covered with the velvet, the edge all round being finished with pale pink, blue and silver tinsel cord. The bag is slightly drawn up and sewn together 2½ inches from the bottom, the upper corner being turned back and tacked, so that the velvet corner is exposed. The front upper corner is also turned down and tacked. Loops of ribbon are sewn to the two upper corners, and loops of cord with tassels to the sides.

No. 2.—POINT LACE.

Full instructions for point lace are given in "The Complete Guide to the Work-Table."

MATERIALS REQUIRED FOR ONE YARD: 8 yards braid, 2 yards pearl edge, 2 skeins thread.

No. 3.—POINT LACE.

MATERIALS REQUIRED FOR 1 YARD: 11½ yards point braid, 2 yards pearl edge, 3 skeins thread.

NO. 1.—FAN-BAG.

PASTIMES.

BURIED PROVERB.

"True friendship's laws are by this rule exprest,
Welcome the coming, speed the parting guest."
Pope.

"Let us, then, be up and doing,
With a heart for any fate."
Longfellow.

"And I oft have heard defended,
Little said is soonest mended."
George Whittier.

"I hold it fit that we shake hands and part,
You, as your business and desires shall point."
Hamlet.

"Still achieving, still pursuing,
Learn to labour and to wait."
Longfellow.

"Care to our coffin adds a nail, no doubt,
And every grin so merry, draws one out."
John Wolcot.

"Do good by stealth and blush to find it fame."
Pope.

"How ill white hairs become a fool and jester."
Henry IV.

SOLUTION OF PASTIMES IN No. 1,660.

CHARADE.—Headline.

THERE is in every town a certain set of busy-bodies who are always moving about in a hurry; very active, though having in reality nothing to do; always in a bustle, though they are really idle; panting without a cause, and in affecting to do much, doing in fact nothing whatever; troublesome to themselves, and a perfect nuisance to others. —*Phædrus.*

NO. 2.—POINT LACE.

NO. 3.—POINT LACE.

The Young Ladies' Journal, March 1896.

DESCRIPTION OF

FANCY WORK,

Continued.

No. 4.—CROCHET: BORDER AND CORNER.

This handsome lace is suitable for inserting in pillow cases, tea-table cloths, sideboard cloths, etc.; a perfect corner is formed in the working, thus preventing the usual gathers. Worked in Evans's 18, or Chadwick's 24 cotton, with a No. 5 steel hook, it makes an insertion 3½ inches wide. It is worked backwards and forwards on a chain of 86 stitches.

1st Row: 3 chain to form 1st treble, 1 treble into next, then 27 times 2 chain, pass over 2, 1 treble into next, 1 treble to finish.

2nd Row: 3 chain, 1 treble, 2 chain, 1 treble, 2 chain, 7 trebles, 2 chain, 4 trebles, 2 chain, 1 treble twice, 2 chain, 4 trebles, 2 chain 1 treble 7 times, [illegible] 5 trebles, 2 chain, 1 treble, 2 chain, 1 treble, 2 chain 4 trebles, 2 chain, 7 trebles, 2 chain, 1 treble, 2 chain, 2 trebles to finish.

3rd Row: 3 chain, 1 treble, 2 chain, 1 treble, 2 chain, 7 trebles, 2 chain, 7 trebles, 2 chain, 1 treble, 2 chain, 7 trebles, 2 chain 1 treble 5 times, then 6 trebles, 2 chain, 1 treble, 2 chain, 7 trebles, 2 chain, 7 trebles, 2 chain, 1 treble, 2 chain, 2 trebles.

4th Row: 3 chain, 1 treble, 2 chain 1 treble 4 times, then 9 trebles, 2 chain, 1 treble, 2 chain, 10 trebles, 2 chain, 1 treble, 2 chain, 1 treble, 2 chain, 10 trebles, 2 chain, 1 treble, 2 chain, 10 trebles, 2 chain 1 treble 4 times, then 1 treble to finish the row.

5th Row: 3 chain, 1 treble, 2 chain, 1 treble, 2 chain, 16 trebles, 2 chain, 1 treble, 2 chain, 13 trebles, 2 chain, 13 trebles, 2 chain, 1 treble, 2 chain, 16 trebles, 2 chain, 1 treble, 2 chain, 2 trebles.

6th Row: 3 chain, 1 treble, 2 chain, 1 treble, 2 chain, 1 treble, 2 chain, 13 trebles, 2 chain, 1 treble, 2 chain, 13 trebles, 2 chain, 13 trebles, 2 chain, 1 treble, 2 chain, 13 trebles, 2 chain 1 treble 3 times, then 1 treble to finish row.

7th Row: 3 chain, 1 treble, 2 chain 1 treble 7 times, 3 trebles, 2 chain, 10 trebles, 2 chain, 4 trebles, 2 chain, 10 trebles, 2 chain, 4 trebles, 2 chain 1 treble 7 times, then 1 treble to finish row.

8th Row: 3 chain, 1 treble, 2 chain 1 treble 8 times, 9 trebles, 2 chain, 1 treble, 2 chain, 4 trebles, 2 chain, 1 treble, 2 chain, 10 trebles, 2 chain 1 treble 8 times, 1 treble to finish.

9th Row: 3 chain, 1 treble, 2 chain, 1 treble, 2 chain, 25 trebles, 2 chain, 1 treble, 2 chain, 1 treble, 2 chain, 4 trebles, 2 chain, 1 treble, 2 chain, 1 treble, 2 chain, 25 trebles, 2 chain, 1 treble, 2 chain, 2 trebles.

10th Row: 3 chain, 1 treble, 2 chain, 1 treble, 2 chain, 1 treble, 2 chain, 19 trebles, 2 chain, 4 trebles, 2 chain, 1 treble, 2 chain, 4 trebles, 2 chain, 1 treble, 2 chain, 4 trebles, 2 chain, 19 trebles, 2 chain, 1 treble, 2 chain, 1 treble, 2 chain, 2 trebles.

11th Row: 3 chain, 1 treble, 2 chain 1 treble 4 times, then 12 trebles, 2 chain 1 treble 3 times, 3 trebles, 2 chain, 4 trebles, 2 chain, 4 trebles, 2 chain 1 treble 3 times, 12 trebles, 2 chain 1 treble 4 times, 1 treble to finish.

12th Row: 3 chain, 1 treble, 2 chain 1 treble 5 times, 6 trebles, 2 chain 1 treble 5 times, 9 trebles, 2 chain 1 treble 5 times, 6 trebles, 2 chain 1 treble 5 times, 1 treble to finish the row.

13th Row: 3 chain, 1 treble, 2 chain 1 treble 7 times, 19 trebles, 2 chain, 19 trebles, 2 chain 1 treble 7 times, 1 treble to finish the row. This is the centre row of the star; make the second half to correspond, of course commencing from the twelfth row, working back to the first row.

In making the corner, beginning with the last row of star previous to the corner star, leave out the 2 chain, 2 trebles at the end, and in each following row in corresponding places; after finishing the corner star work one extra row of holes, and over this last row of holes, 1 double into each treble, 2 chain; repeat all along this to simulate the two trebles of edge. Break off, and commence with first row along the plain side, working as directed above.

NO. 4.—CROCHET: BORDER AND CORNER.

NO. 5.—TOILET-BOX.

NO. 6.—HAT OR CLOTHES-BRUSH POCKET.

No. 5.—TOILET-BOX.

The foundation of this pretty box is a cigar-box, which should first be lined with a thin sheet of wadding round the inside; above this a slightly gathered piece of pongee silk, with a little tuck at the top, is put in. Next cover a piece of wadding the exact size of the bottom with silk, and gum it in, hiding the edges of the sides and ends, and making all quite neat. The outside of the box is covered with the silk without wadding; it is put on quite plainly, and laid just under the little tuck of the lining, and made firm with a few stitches here and there. Next sew a lace flounce, rather full, and about half an inch less deep than the box, entirely round it. The lid of the box is padded well with wadding to form a pincushion. Silk, a trifle more than half the width of the box, is gathered round the inside and drawn up full with a little tuck in the centre. The inside of the lid is now covered with a piece of wadding covered with silk, which should be fastened on with seccotine, and the inside will then be quite neat. A ruche of ribbon edges the lid; this should be about 1½ inch wide. The centre is ornamented with a bunch of artificial flowers mixed with some loops of ribbon like that of the ruche.

No. 6.—HAT OR CLOTHES-BRUSH POCKET.

This is a handy little pocket to hang beside the hat-stand. The foundation is of stout millboard with a ring sewn on at the top; it is covered with felt, worked over with knot-stitches; the felt is coffee-brown; the stitches are of gold silk; the edge is pinked; the pocket which holds the brush is of light brown cloth, embroidered and sewn to the felt, this also is pinked at the top; a bow of ribbon is put on above it, and cord with tassels ornament the sides; the size of the pocket and foundation must be regulated by the size of the brush for which it is required.

PARIS FASHIONS.

DEAR EVELYN,

Since you have several dinners and evening parties, and not a few concerts to go to before the end of the season, I will mention some toilets from which I think you may be able to choose something to your taste. And first let me say that I am so pleased you have changed your coiffure, and find it an improvement. I am sure the waved and puffed bandeaux and low chignon must be very becoming to your style of face. You will require very little ornament for your hair; a pretty jewelled comb, fancy pins, or a string of pearls are sufficient for the comparatively quiet parties of the beginning of Lent.

Apropos of pearls, I know you have some very good ones, and can give you a few hints as to the way of making use of them. You might have a necklace made up in the latest fashion, which is to have it to fit quite close round the neck in five or six rows, fastened together at regular distances by long clasps of chiselled silver. A silver comb for the chignon, set with pearls, also looks very pretty, and I have seen both worn with a white silk dress, the front of which was embroidered with pearls. This dress is one of those I wished to describe. The bodice is half low and square, plain front and back, but with draperies of white chiffon on each side from the shoulders, and crossed at the waist under a silver belt. The side widths of the white silk skirt are divided from those of the front and back by robings of white chiffon, and the robing on the right side of the front is finished at the top by a spray of white lilies; another syray of the same blossoms is placed near the left shoulder. The loose white silk sleeves open over a drapery of white chiffon. None but pearl and silver ornaments should be worn with this dress, which is beautifully chaste and graceful.

Another pretty dress, suitable for a concert or dinner-party or the opera, is of "libellule" blue and white shot glacé silk. The skirt, plain in front and very clinging about the hips, with godet pleats at the back only, has no trimming. The plain bodice is trimmed with strips of white lace insertion, and finished with a pleated round bertha of white chiffon, embroidered with blue silk and silver spangles, and edged with white lace. The bodice is edged round the waist with blue and white silk cord, a long string of which fastens a white feather fan on the right side. The full drooping sleeves, to the elbow, are of embroidered chiffon, edged with lace to match the berthe. The bodice is only half low, and a "dog's collar" of silver, inlaid with pearls, is worn round the neck.

This is a pretty toilet, youthful and elegant. You will perhaps prefer, however, this other one,

The Young Ladies' Journal, March 1896.

1st row: Button hooks
1. USA; celluloid, probably piece in combination sewing and dresser set. $10.00.
2. USA; steel; c. 1920, $3.00.
3. England; agate handle, clothing hook; c. 1900, $25.00.
4. USA; silver-plate clothing hook; c. 1910, $10.00.
5. England; mother-of-pearl handle, clothing button hook; c. 1900, $10.00.
6., 7. USA; steel, glove or shoe hooks; c. 1910, $4.00.
8. USA; steel, decorative handle, glove hook; c. 1915, $10.00.

2nd row: Bodkins
Left:
1., – 5. Bone bodkins; c. 1900, $5.00 – 15.00.
6. Sterling Webster Company; c. 1915, $50.00.
Center:
USA; set of sterling Webster Company bodkins in silk faille folding case, silk ribbon; c. 1900, $200.00.
Right top:
1. England; steel, elastic threader; c. 1900, $12.00.
2. England; brass, stamped "Queen Bess" "Elastic threader made in England"; c. 1910, $15.00.
3. England; steel, stamped "made in England"; c. 1900, $5.00.
4. USA; flat, steel, Pat. Mar 25 1902; $7.50.
5. England; steel; c. 1900, $4.00.
6. USA; bone; c. 1910, $4.00.
Right lower:
1., 4. England; needle bodkins, steel; c. 1900, $4.00.
2. USA; flat steel, stamped "Singer Souvenir, Panama Exposition 1915", $15.00.
3. Steel sizer guide, stamped "the Dot"; c. 1910, $3.00.

3rd row: Punches, stilleto, and awl
1. USA; gold fill handle, steel shaft; c. 1920, $15.00.
2. USA; stiletto, sterling, Webster Co; 6"; c. 1900, $60.00.
3. England; mother-of-pearl handle, steel shaft; c. 1890, $15.00.
4. – 6. England; bone; c. 1880 – 1900, $5.00 – 10.00.
7. USA; gold fill handle, ivory punch; c. 1880, $10.00.
8. – 11. England; bone; c. 1880 – 1900, $5.00 – 10.00.
12. USA, bone awl stamped "Barnes CO; Lexington Hsp"; c. 1920, $10.00.

Chapter Nine

Thread Holders and Sewing Clamps

The term "thread holder," in its broad meaning, includes anything from the small handmade wooden winder to the ornate, tiered iron stand embellished with mythical characters. Germany was the leading manufacturer of novelty thread holders. The souvenir industry in Scotland, where there were many thread manufacturers, adapted transfer ware, tartan ware, and fern transfer boxes to thread holders. Clark & Co. as well as other thread manufacturers printed a label inside the thread box (see page 125). These boxes had spindles to hold the thread in place and ivory eyelets to allow the thread to come out of the box without having to remove it.

Small pierced and plain ivory holders were often part of a lacemaking toolbox. Figurative holders of bears, barrels, horses, and dogs were popular and often used as decoration in the Victorian parlor.

The packaging and display of thread at the beginning of the twentieth century signaled the decline of home sewing. Paper boxes, rather than attractive wooden boxes and large spool cabinets, were now used to display thread and attract the buyer. Spool cabinets were converted to household items and disappeared from the general store.

England; ivory holders.

1. Pierced work of flowers, shields, both top and post unscrew; 3½"; c. 1875, $75.00.
2. Carving overall is tall ferns, top pierced to hold six needles anchored in cork, the thread holder unscrews at the center; 4¼"; c. 1875, $100.00.
3. Simple carving circling the barrel; 2"; c. 1875, $65.00.

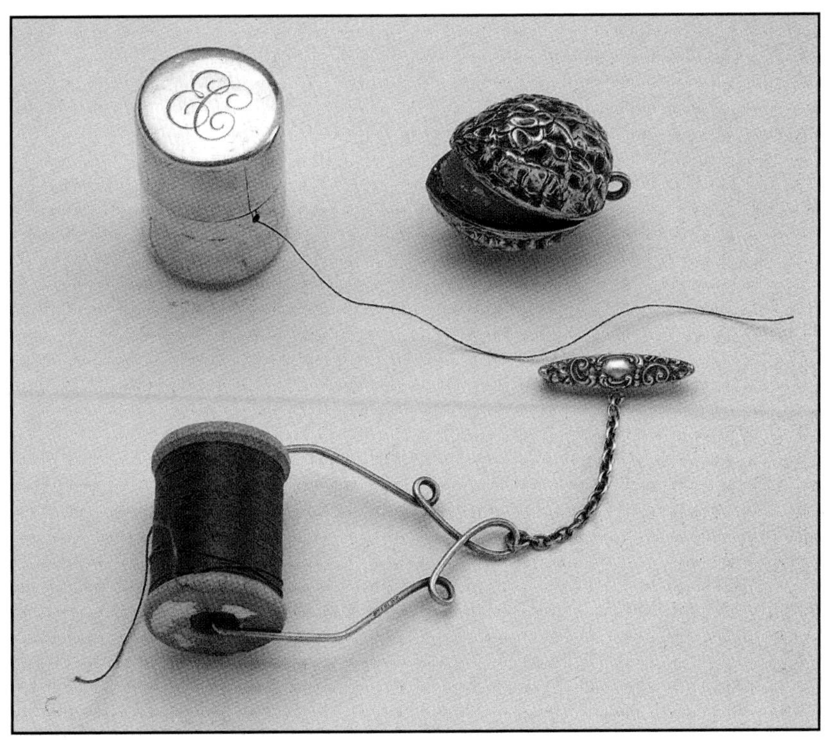

1st row:

1. USA; single spool thread holder marked sterling, 3791 with rose spray; 1" x 1½"; c. 1915, $85.00.
2. USA; sterling acorn beeswax holder with ring and wax; 1" x 1½"; c. 1875, $125.00.

2nd row:

3. USA; sterling spool holder with lapel pin, pin and tongs marked "sterling"; see page 71; 4"; c. 1915, $135.00.

1st row:

1. Germany; thread box with spindles, painted and floral decal; 2" x 4½"; c. 1900, $75.00.
2. New York, USA; architectural thread and yarn holder, walnut with mother-of-pearl key hole in drawer; 5½" x 9½"; c. 1890, $850.00.
3. USA; walnut thread stand with drawer, pincushion, and thimble spindle; 4" x 6½"; c. 1900, $125.00.

2nd row:

1. USA; painted metal thread and thimble holder; 3" x 2"; c. 1920, $30.00.
2. USA; wood-round with bark thread holder with pincushion, and thimble spindle; 4½" x 2½"; c. 1920, $45.00.
3. New York, USA; sweet grass thread holder with top made by Native Americans; 1¾" x 3¾"; c. 1900, $65.00.

3rd row:

1. USA; cardboard box with thirteen ⅝" spools of silk thread, hand-lettered and painted top decal reads "Take me with you on a trip, I may prove handy to mend a rip"; 1¾" x 2"; c. 1900, $15.00.

USA; South Carolina; maker unknown, mahogany with maple inlay and brass pull, this is a wall piece, hangs from back facing; 19" x 7½" x 5".

Front of the cabinet swings down and stops on a rest, making it functional when needed for sewing and a decorative piece when closed. This piece was made from early 1800 wood; c. 1920, $125.00.

Top row:

1. German; bear of carved wood, carries thimble on paw, needles in bucket on his back, and stands above the spools of thread; c. 1880, $110.00.
2. USA; with pincushion and storage drawer, spindles for thread, mahogany; c. 1880, $95.00.
3. England; pewter; c. 1875, $200.00.
4. England; walnut, maple trim pincushion and storage drawer; c. 1875, $110.00.
5. USA; wrought iron thread stand with eight spindles and velvet pincushion; c. 1875, $75.00.

2nd row:

1. England; Machline transfer ware on wood, four spindles inside and four ivory eyelets on side of box; c. 1880, $70.00.
2. German; carved wooden bear, sitting; c. 1890, $120.00.

3rd row:

1. USA; thread saver, Shaker style, leather with silk ribbon; c. 1900, $65.00.
2. England; painted tin Clark's thread box; c. 1890, $20.00.

England; Machline transfer ware; top of box Dr. Livingston and Henry M. Stanley touching medallions; front and back of box have three thread size labels over the three ivory eyelets; inside there are dowels for six spools (one missing), there are lifts on four of the dowels, each a different size; inside the box lid is a Clark's label "O.N.T." in each corner, egg shape medallion displaying reproductions of eight medallions won at European Expositions 1862, 1867; "use Clark's spool cotton, George A. Clark, sole agent"; below the front eyelet says "made of wood which grew near Alloway Kirk, on banks of Doon," sycamore wood; c. 1880, $200.00.

1. Ireland; wood spool for linen thread, label "York Street Threads Ltd, made in N. Ireland, linen thread. Belfast N. Ireland"; $4.00.
2. USA; colonial lady wood cut-out with balance platform and spindle for thread in back, painted with relief flowers; hole for thread to come back to front center left side; 8"; c. 1915, $20.00.

1. Asia; ivory thread canister, screw top, edge of top pierced and fluted, possibly came out of a lacemaker's box; c. 1865, $140.00.
2. USA; wood desk-style thread holder, slant top lifts, ink well a thimble holder; c. 1925, $25.00.

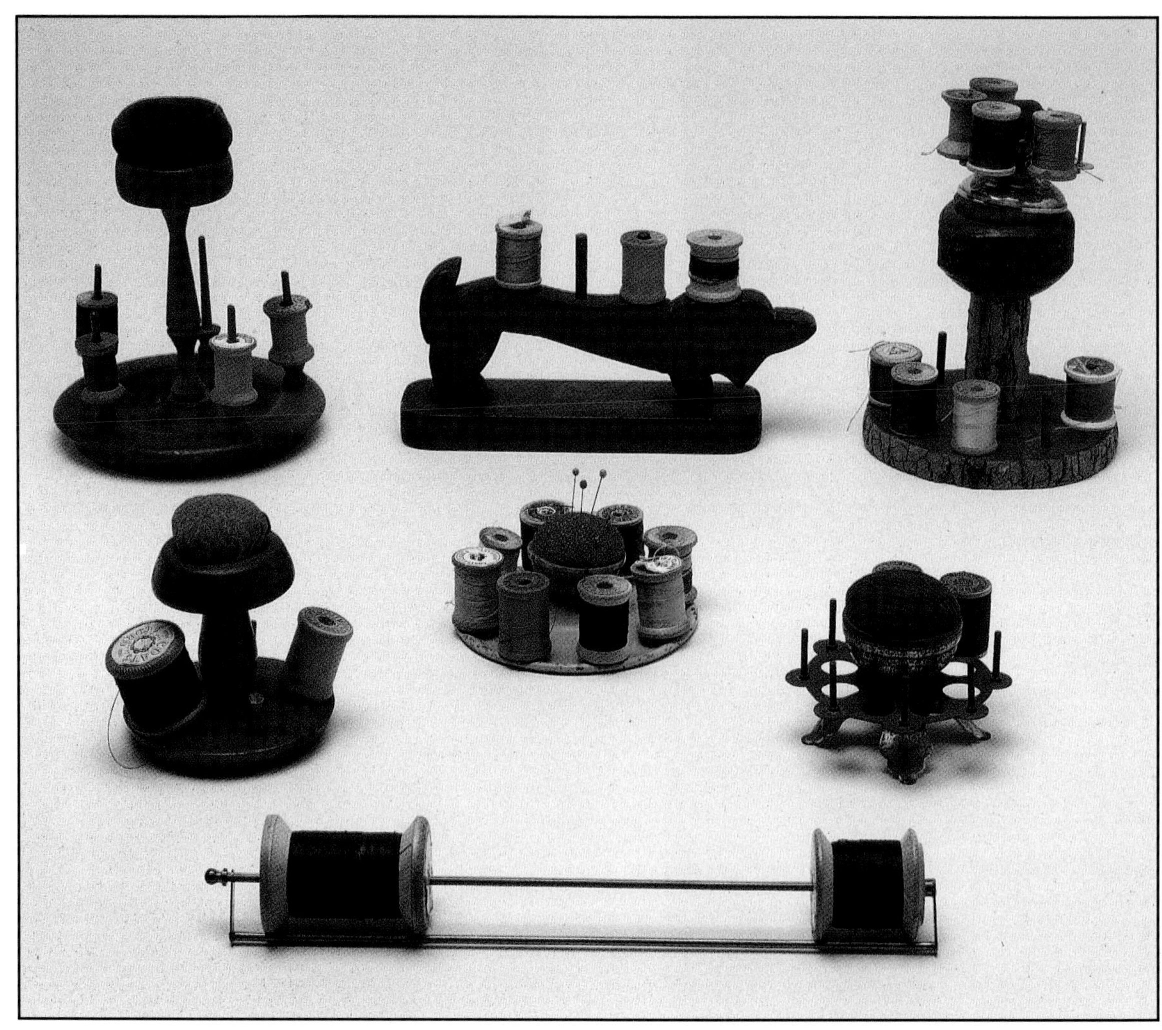

Top row:

1. USA; holder with pincushion and tray, made of poplar wood; c. 1910, $30.00.
2. USA; dachshund, wood; c. 1930, $15.00.
3. USA; stand made of birch, souvenir Michigan; c. 1920, $20.00.

3a. USA; carousel, six spindles and pincushion, polished metal; c. 1925, $20.00.

2nd row:

1. USA; wood, souvenir "Evansville"; c. 1935, $15.00.
2. USA; painted metal, eight spindles, pincushion; c. 1935, $28.00.
3. USA; eight spindle thread well, polished metal; c. 1930, $15.00.

3rd row:

1. England; rare, brass; c. 1890, $65.00.

USA; black iron thread display with folding stand; c. 1900, $75.00.

USA; walnut, refinished, brass pulls, company unknown; $350.00.

Willimantic; four drawers, walnut, all original, decals on side; $950.00.

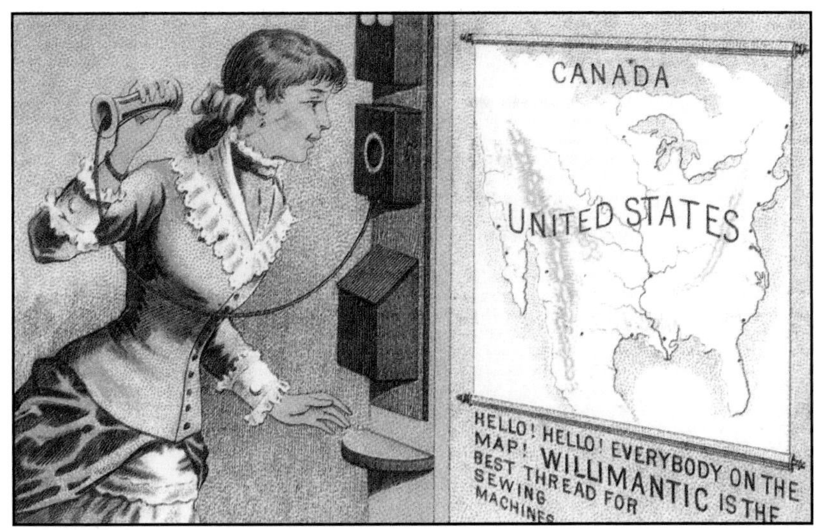

Paper ad, front and back.

USA; Merrick; oak, four full drawers, two half drawers, completely refinished (had black lettering before being refinished); $450.00.

USA; J&P Coats, walnut, anchor-shaped brass pulls, original decals on sides and back, old tin decals replaced with new on drawers; $1,400.00.

1. This refinished J&P Coats chest matches the original on page 130, $1,000.00.

2. The original brass pulls inscribed with the company logo.

3. The decals on the side are of original design, but repainted.

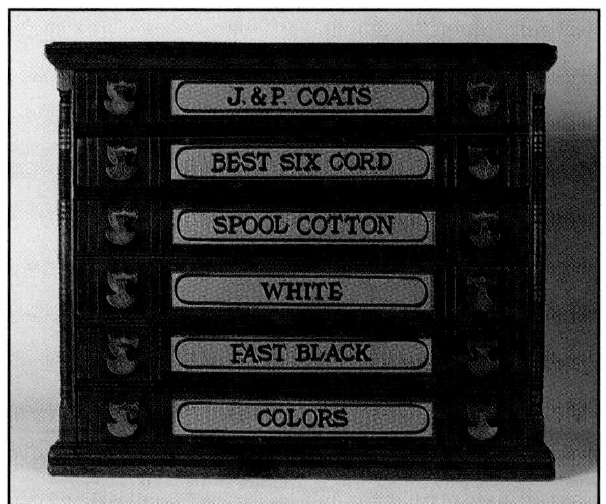

1.

2.

3.

Refinished J. & P. Coats spool chest, walnut, note the beautiful decorative designs behind each brass pull; $950.00.

USA; Eureka four-drawer thread cabinet, white china pulls, original, excellent condition; $500.00.

Brooks Thread card.

Trading cards, paper; $2.00 – $10.00.

Top row:

1. J&P Coats thread, "Choose the best Shade"; c. 1900.
2. Clark's O.N.T. Spool Cotton, "TESTING"; c. 1900.

2nd row:

1., 2. J&P Coats

    1. c. 1915.
    2. Copy of early domestic scene; 1900.

3 .– 5. Clarks' ONT; c. 1890 – 1910.

3rd row:

1. Merrick Thread Co., finest six cord; c. 1910.
2. Dressmaker's ad with J&P Coats on the back.
3. Eureka Spool Silk in Vermont store ad; hand painted.

4th row:

1. J&P Coats, "The Champion"; c. 1890.
2. – 5. Willamantic; c. 1890.

Clamps

The thumb screw hemming clamp was an important sewing tool by the eighteenth century. Fabric sewing projects, large or small, could be anchored between the table top and the clamp stand when tightening the thumb screw. Gay Ann Rogers in ***Illustrated History of Needlework Tools*** writes that the sewing clamp was known as "third hands." The addition of the pincushion, thread winders, and needle holders expanded the versatility of the clamp.

There were also lacemaking and netting clamps. Large early clamps were made of iron and cut steel. As in most of the sewing tools, the second half of the nineteenth century manufacturers offered a more diversified selection of clamps in design and materials. Wooden clamps are usually interesting and attractive (pages 135 and 136).

The figural clamps of this period continue to be popular with collectors.

The hollow, stamped brass sewing bird was preceded by the 1750 solid iron bird that is a much simpler stylized design and has no pincushion. Charles Waterman patented the brass sewing bird in February, 1853. His design did not have feathers stamped on the under body, had a plain, undecorated clamp, and had one small emery-filled pincushion on the bird's back. Variations of the sewing bird were manufactured continually into the 1930s and reproductions have been available since the 1980s. Manufacturers were able to comply with existing patent laws with slight variations in body designs, number and placement of pincushions, and other accessories that became a part of the function of the sewing bird. By pressing down on the tail of the sewing bird the beak becomes the clamp to hold a fabric project in place when sewing.

Clamps continue to be of interest to both the casual and serious collectors.

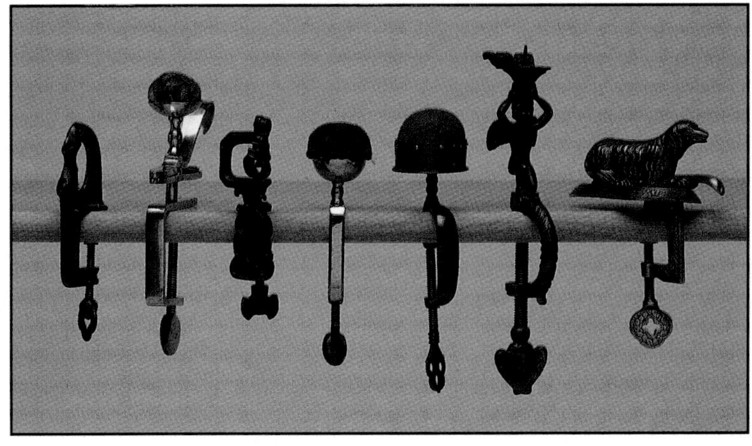

1. England; iron goose, front piece under the beak has a spring action that is pushed down in order to place fabric between and grip it in preparing to sew; c. 1780, $250.00.
2. England; cut steel, new pincushion cover, 1875 fabric, the handle behind the pincushion is pressed down to open the fabric clamp; c. 1840, $175.00–$225.00.
3. England; cast iron, scroll-style decorative design, the fan-shaped arm swings to one side to put the fabric in place to secure for sewing; c. 1840, $150.00–$190.00.
4. England; cut steel, velvet pincushion with braid trim, initials "AE" etched on the thumb screw of the clamp; c. 1850, $110.00–$140.00.
5. England; cast iron, wool covered pincushion held in cup with heavy straight pins placed from the side; c. 1790, $225.00–$300.00.
6. England; cast iron, originally had a gilt finish, half of the lily leaf platform broken off, thumb screw is a Cupid surrounded by wings on both sides, Cupid supporting platform; c. 1850, $175.00.
7. England; dog, molded brass, the dog is two hollow halves joined with a brass pin behind the front legs, the lever between the front legs is solid brass, when pressed the lower iron jaw opens; c. 1850, $1,000.00.

Sewing Birds

1. England; iron, heart thumb screw, the bird is 3½" long; c. 1790, $200.00.
2. England; gilted brass cast, stamped "Patented 1853" under the tail; $300.00.
3. Cast brass, stamped under pincushion mounting "Norton's Improved Patent applied for May 1853," crosshatch design on top of bird, smooth under body; 3¾"; $300.00.
4. USA; brass; lower pincushion missing, stamped "Patented" on one wing, "Feb. 15, 1853" on the second wing, designs on under body; bird 3¾"; $125.00.
5., 6. Silver over brass, original pin cushions on #5 shows wear, under body has overall design, stamped "Patented" "Feb 15, 1853"; $250.00 – $325.00.

1. England; heavily carved wood, the nap has worn off the velvet cushion; 6"; c. 1840, $125.00–$175.00.
2. England; walnut, natural finish, pincushion cover brown & tan cotton print; 6½"; c. 1850, $150.00–$195.00.
3. USA; varnished wood, embroidery hoop missing (see page 136); 6¼"; c. 1860. NPA.
4. Scotland; transfer ware on wood, country scene, velvet cushion; 8"; c. 1860, $100.00–$200.00.
5. Yarn winders, used in pairs, can be dismantled by unscrewing the ball cup, remove the cage and unscrew the center post; 6½"; c. 1875, $250.00 – $350.00.

England; painted wood clamp with iron thumb screw, decorated with mirror; 2½" x 5½"; c. 1875, $180.00.

1. England; disc shape, wood, hand-rubbed walnut, velvet cushion, shield-shape thumbscrew; c. 1860, $150.00.
2. England; hand-carved walnut, velvet cushion; c. 1860, $165.00.
3. USA; emboridery hoop and clamp, hoop telescopes into hole in the top of the clamp, wood; c. 1875, $75.00–$100.00.

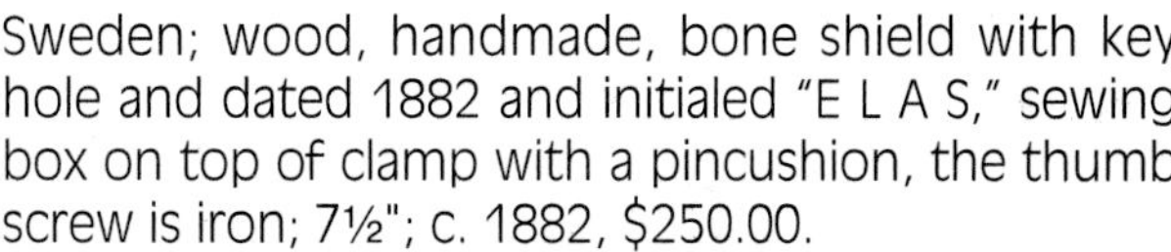

Sweden; wood, handmade, bone shield with key hole and dated 1882 and initialed "E L A S," sewing box on top of clamp with a pincushion, the thumb screw is iron; 7½"; c. 1882, $250.00.

J.& P. COATS
COLORS

Chapter Ten

Sewing Machines

The development of the sewing machine was accomplished through the efforts of many inventors. According to Victor Houart, in his book entitled "Sewing Accessories, An Illustrated History", an eighteenth century Englishman named Thomas Saint patented a crude stitching device that was never successful. No one knew about this machine until approximately 100 years after its creation when the patent was discovered in the cupboards of the British patent office. In the patent application, Saint's invention was described as "a quilting, stitching, and sewing machine."

In 1830, Barthemey Thimonnier of France patented a working, wooden, mechanized, chainstitch sewing machine. After improvements were made to the machine, a workshop was set up in Paris to mass produce French Army uniforms with Thimonnier acting as supervisor. The economic and political climate of the time generated a mob reaction by the producers of handmade clothing (tailors, etc.) who were threatened by Thimonnier's achievement. The mob destroyed the machines and the building that housed the workshop. In the United States, two independent inventors, Walter Hunt of New York and Elias Howe of Massachusetts, were working on the development of a sewing machine with a lock stitch. Although Hunt's work preceded Howe, he delayed his application until 1852, when he was turned down because Howe had already been granted a patent. During the middle of the nineteenth century, there were many improvements made to the sewing machine. Many individuals, the most famous being Isaac Singer, were using Howe's invention without his knowledge or approval. Howe took them to court, and as a result, a patent pool was established in order to settle disputes and compensate Howe. By 1860, the Singer Sewing Machine Company was the largest producer and distributor of sewing machines, with over 110,000 machines sold that year. Singer introduced the treadle which gave the sewer more control over a work in progress. Treadle machines are still used today, with China the largest producer. It is interesting to note that Japan introduced the versatile zig-zag innovation to the sewing machine. Companies also produced miniature and small machines for women and girls. Many collectors have enjoyed discovering these treasures.

Walter Hunt of New York was a very talented and successful inventor. The safety pin was one of his inventions, as well as the cloth covered cardboard collar for men, which was popular into the early twentieth century.

There are a number of museums with sewing machines included in their collections. Two that are highly recommended are Clydebank Museum, Clydebank Town Hall, Scotland, and the Thimonnier Museum in Lyon, France.

USA; Singer Manufacturing Company; treadle in a beautiful Art Deco walnut cabinet, note the excellent gold and red decorative work; oak attachment box and attachments on the stand; c. 1920, $180.00.

This portrait of a York, Pennsylvania, family and the mother/wife's Singer sewing machine represents the importance of new lock stitch machines for family sewing after 1865.

USA; Singer Automatic, treadle base, this machine was built for about 40 years beginning in 1890; early models had flower transfers instead of the geometric designs as seen here, there is an electric portable that has the same look with an instruction book dated 1920; 1932; $150.00.

USA; National Sewing Machine Company, Belvidere, Illinois, chain stitch; c. 1920, $100.00.

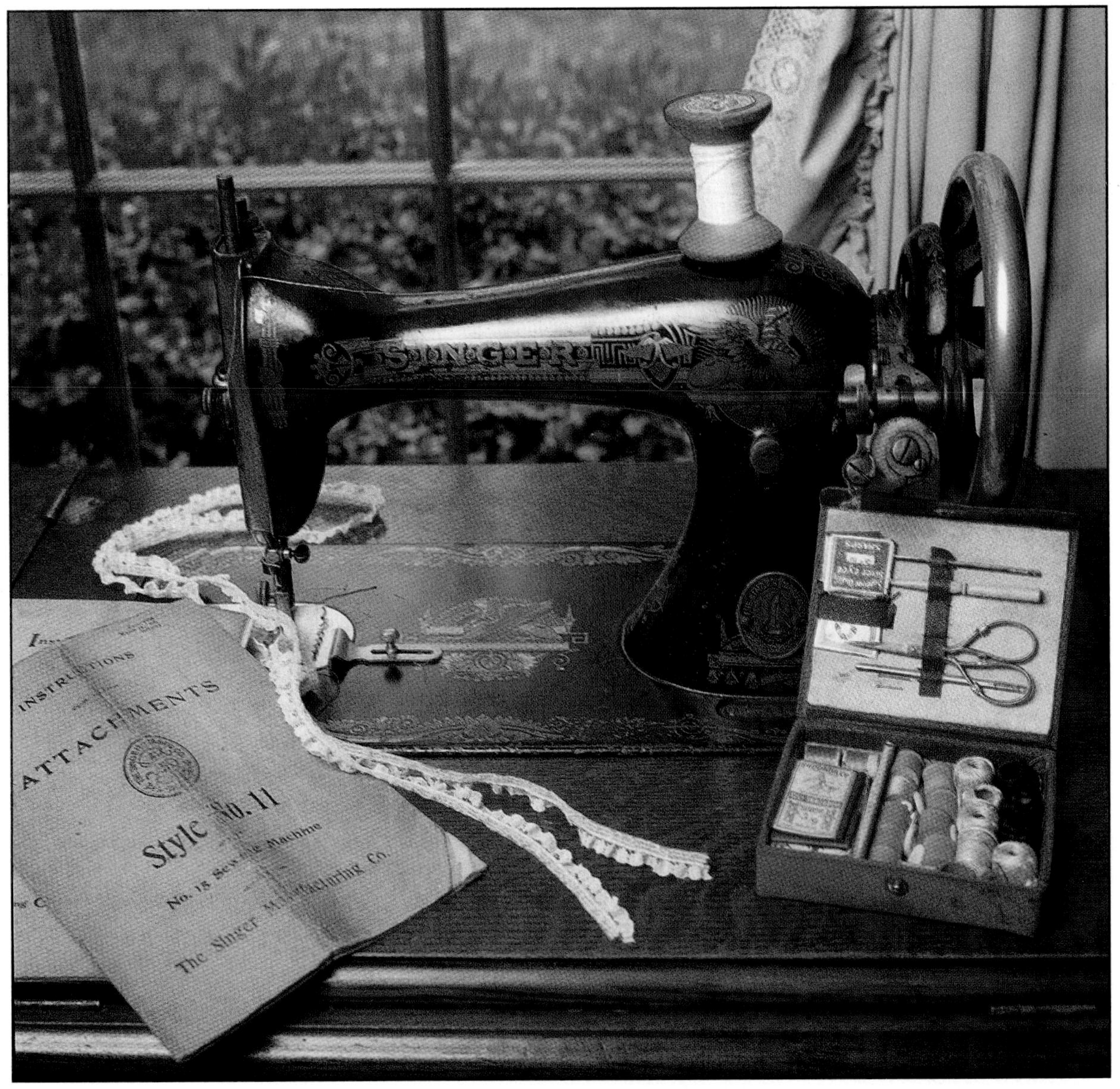

1. USA; Singer treadle machine in its oak cabinet, working order and excellent condition, patent dates on sewing plate, attachment instructions, number 15 machine, beautiful gold designs; c. 1875, $250.00.
2. Sewing box; c. 1920, $10.00.

USA; Singer, chain stitch, very good condition, beautiful floral designs on sewing plate as well as body of machine; c.1910, $75.00.

Germany; toy machine, FW Muller, #19; c. 1927, $200.00.

"ATLAS" LOCK-STITCH SEWING MACHINE. 39/-

Equal in size and quality to any Machine. The best and cheapest for every use. Works by Hand or Treadle. 4 years' guarantee. To ensure satisfaction, we will send Machine on receipt of 5/- P.O. for one month's trial. Balance can be paid

5/- MONTHLY.

CALL OR SEND FOR DESIGNS & SAMPLES OF WORK.
THE ATLAS CO., 184, High Street, Camden Town, London; 63, Seven Sisters Road; 14, High Road, Kilburn, N.W.

The Young Ladies' Journal, March 1896.

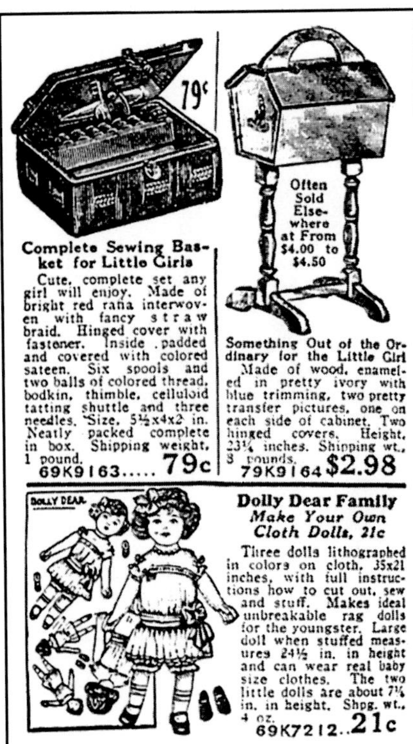

79¢
Complete Sewing Basket for Little Girls
Cute, complete set any girl will enjoy. Made of bright red rafia interwoven with fancy straw braid. Hinged cover with fastener. Inside padded and covered with colored sateen. Six spools and two balls of colored thread, bodkin, thimble, celluloid tatting shuttle and three needles. Size, 5½x4x2 in. Neatly packed complete in box. Shipping weight, 1 pound.
69K9163..... 79c
Often Sold Elsewhere at From $4.00 to $4.50
Something Out of the Ordinary for the Little Girl
Made of wood, enameled in pretty ivory with blue trimming, two pretty transfer pictures, one on each side of cabinet. Two hinged covers. Height, 23¼ inches. Shipping wt., 8 pounds.
79K9164 $2.98
DOLLY DEAR
Dolly Dear Family
Make Your Own Cloth Dolls, 21c
Three dolls lithographed in colors on cloth, 35x21 inches, with full instructions how to cut out, sew and stuff. Makes ideal unbreakable rag dolls for the youngster. Large doll when stuffed measures 24½ in. in height and can wear real baby size clothes. The two little dolls are about 7¼ in. in height. Shpg. wt., 4 oz.
69K7212..21c

Sears, Roebuck & Co., 1927. Girls were conditioned early with role model tools as toys.

LADIES! DO NOT FAIL

to send at once for design showing exact size of **W. J. HARRIS & Co.'s unrivalled DEFIANCE LOCK-STITCH SEWING MACHINE,** works by hand or treadle,

ONLY 45s. COMPLETE.

Four Years' Warranty with each Machine. Thousands in use.

Admired and praised by everyone.

Especially adapted for Dressmaking, Light Tailoring, and all kinds of Family Sewing, and so simple as to require no instructions beyond the Guide Book, which is given, and all accessories, with each Machine.

Sent to any part of the Country on easy terms, 5/. per month. Full particulars post free.

W. J. HARRIS & Co., Limited,

219, Old Kent Road, S.E.; 69, Newington Causeway, S.E.; 62, Powis Street, Woolwich; 66, London Street, Greenwich; 391, Mare Street, Hackney, London, E.; and Branches.

The Young Ladies' Journal, March 1896.

Sears, Roebuck and Co. ad, 1927.

1st row:

1. Germany; Muller, decorative floral transfer, clamp and box; c. 1920, $200.00.
2. Singer on base; c. 1885, $300.00.
   Singer oil can; $5.00.
3. Germany; tin plate, on sewing plate "an eagle over the name Casige," the name appears at each end of the base; story book character transfer on both sides; $180.00.

2nd row:

1. Germany; tinplate; transfer design,"made in Germany British Zone"; c. 1950, $175.00.
2. New Jersey, USA; Singer; single thread elastic chain stitch, cast metal; c. 1910, $200.00.
3. USA; Singer; cast metal, brown, SewHandy, model 20, instruction book and needle pack; c. 1950, $150.00.
4. Germany; Muller; small machine, transfer ware yellow flowers and leaves, tinplate, #450 280 on sewing plate, thread on machine Singer Sewing Machine Company, Ltd, held on spindle with screw, washer, and spring; c. 1910, $220.00.
5. USA; Singer; cast metal, SewHandy model 20, black; c. 1950, $125.00.

USA; adjustable pattern plates for drafting garments, A. McDowell Pattern Drafting Machine Co, New York City, Patent 1879, brass (also available with nickel plate), along with adjustable patterns (five pieces) is an instruction book, square measure, measuring book, tracing wheel, each piece of each full pattern is ruled off in inches, at each joining there is a screw for adjustments, each pattern piece is marked with patent dates; 1879, $100.00.

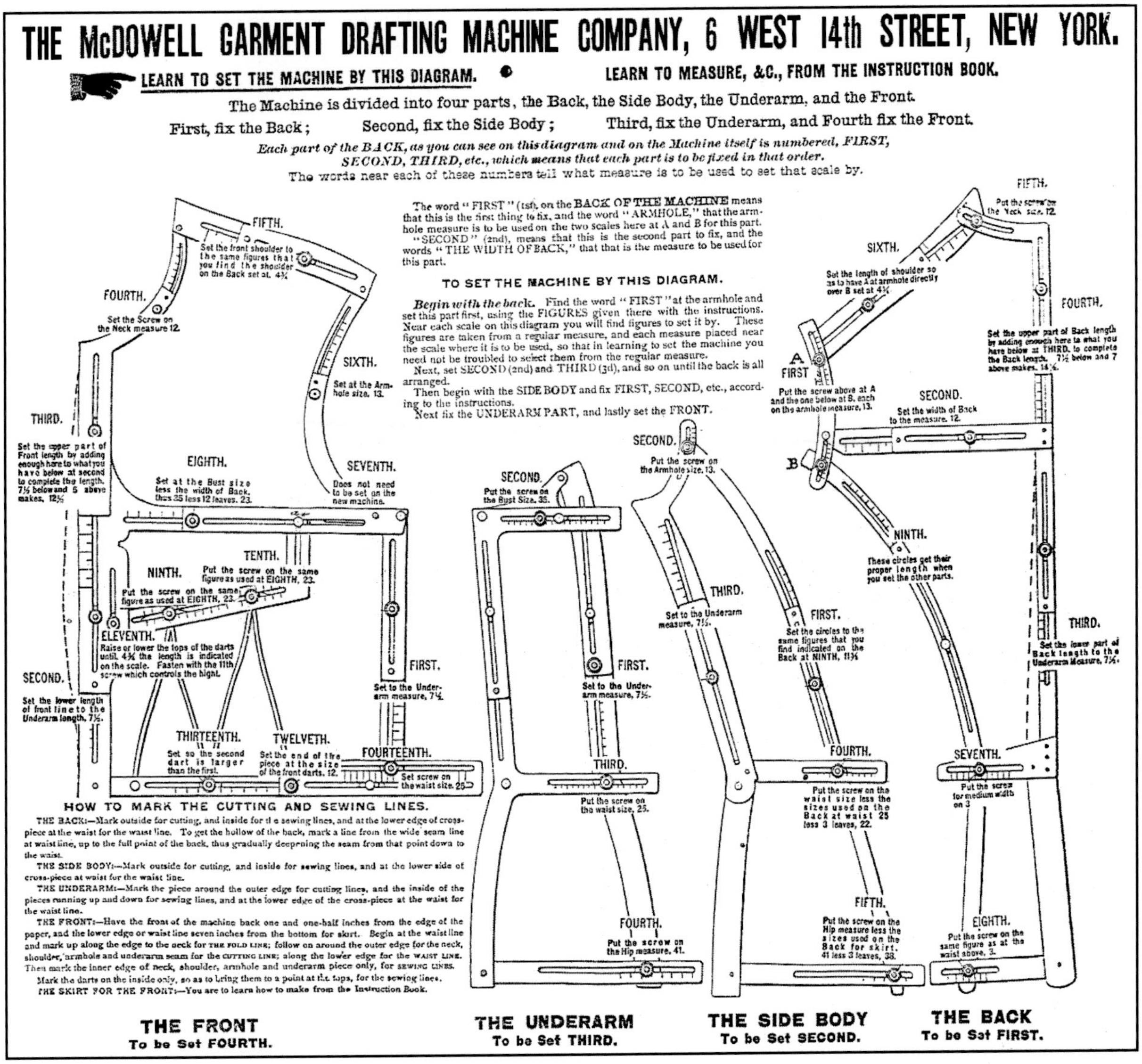

THE McDOWELL GARMENT DRAFTING MACHINE COMPANY, 6 WEST 14th STREET, NEW YORK.

LEARN TO SET THE MACHINE BY THIS DIAGRAM. • **LEARN TO MEASURE, &C., FROM THE INSTRUCTION BOOK.**

The Machine is divided into four parts, the Back, the Side Body, the Underarm, and the Front.

First, fix the Back; Second, fix the Side Body; Third, fix the Underarm, and Fourth fix the Front.

Each part of the BACK, as you can see on this diagram and on the Machine itself is numbered, FIRST, SECOND, THIRD, etc., which means that each part is to be fixed in that order.

The words near each of these numbers tell what measure is to be used to set that scale by.

The word "FIRST" (1st), on the BACK OF THE MACHINE means that this is the first thing to fix, and the word "ARMHOLE," that the armhole measure is to be used on the two scales here at A and B for this part.

"SECOND" (2nd), means that this is the second part to fix, and the words "THE WIDTH OF BACK," that that is the measure to be used for this part.

TO SET THE MACHINE BY THIS DIAGRAM.

Begin with the back. Find the word "FIRST" at the armhole and set this part first, using the FIGURES given there with the instructions. Near each scale on this diagram you will find figures to set it by. These figures are taken from a regular measure, and each measure placed near the scale where it is to be used, so that in learning to set the machine you need not be troubled to select them from the regular measure.

Next, set SECOND (2nd) and THIRD (3d), and so on until the back is all arranged.

Then begin with the SIDE BODY and fix FIRST, SECOND, etc., according to the instructions.

Next fix the UNDERARM PART, and lastly set the FRONT.

FIFTH. Set the front shoulder to the same figures that you find the shoulder on the Back set at. 4¾
FOURTH. Set the Screw on the Neck measure 12.
SIXTH. Set at the Armhole size. 13.
THIRD. Set the upper part of Front length by adding enough here to what you have below at second to complete the length. 7½ below and 5 above makes. 12½
EIGHTH. Set at the Bust size less the width of Back, thus 35 less 12 leaves. 23.
SEVENTH. Does not need to be set on the new machine.
TENTH.
NINTH. Put the screw on the same figure as used at EIGHTH, 23.
Put the screw on the same figure as used at EIGHTH, 23.
ELEVENTH. Raise or lower the tops of the darts until 4¾ the length is indicated on the scale. Fasten with the 11th screw which controls the hight.
SECOND. Set the lower length of front line to the Underarm length. 7½.
FIRST. Set to the Underarm measure, 7½.
THIRTEENTH. Set so the second dart is larger than the first.
TWELVETH. Set the end of the piece at the size of the front darts. 12.
FOURTEENTH. Set screw on the waist size. 25

SECOND. Put the screw on the Bust Size. 35.
FIRST. Set to the Underarm measure, 7½.
THIRD. Put the screw on the waist size, 25.
FOURTH. Put the screw on the Hip measure, 41.

SECOND. Put the screw on the Armhole size. 13.
THIRD. Set to the Underarm measure, 7½.
FIRST. Set the circles to the same figures that you find indicated on the Back at NINTH, 11⅜
FOURTH. Put the screw on the waist size less the sizes used on the Back at waist 25 less 3 leaves, 22.
FIFTH. Put the screw on the Hip measure less the sizes used on the Back for skirt. 41 less 3 leaves, 38.

FIFTH. Put the screw on the Neck size. 12.
SIXTH. Set the length of shoulder so as to have A at armhole directly over B set at 4¾
FOURTH. Set the upper part of Back length by adding enough here to what you have below at THIRD, to complete the Back length. 7½ below and 7 above makes. 14¼.
A FIRST. Put the screw above at A and the one below at B, each on the armhole measure, 13.
SECOND. Set the width of Back to the measure, 12.
B
NINTH. These circles get their proper length when you set the other parts.
THIRD. Set the lower part of Back length to the Underarm Measure, 7½.
SEVENTH. Put the screw for medium width on 3
EIGHTH. Put the screw on the same figure as at the waist above, 3.

HOW TO MARK THE CUTTING AND SEWING LINES.

THE BACK:—Mark outside for cutting, and inside for the sewing lines, and at the lower edge of cross-piece at the waist for the waist line. To get the hollow of the back, mark a line from the wide seam line at waist line, up to the full point of the back, thus gradually deepening the seam from that point down to the waist.

THE SIDE BODY:—Mark outside for cutting, and inside for sewing lines, and at the lower side of cross-piece at waist for the waist line.

THE UNDERARM:—Mark the piece around the outer edge for cutting lines, and the inside of the pieces running up and down for sewing lines, and at the lower edge of the cross-piece at the waist for the waist line.

THE FRONT:—Have the front of the machine back one and one-half inches from the edge of the paper, and the lower edge or waist line seven inches from the bottom for skirt. Begin at the waist line and mark up along the edge to the neck for THE FOLD LINE; follow on around the outer edge for the neck, shoulder, armhole and underarm seam for the CUTTING LINE; along the lower edge for the WAIST LINE. Then mark the inner edge of neck, shoulder, armhole and underarm piece only, for SEWING LINES.

Mark the darts on the inside only, so as to bring them to a point at the tops, for the sewing lines.

THE SKIRT FOR THE FRONT:—You are to learn how to make from the Instruction Book.

THE FRONT To be Set FOURTH.

THE UNDERARM To be Set THIRD.

THE SIDE BODY To be Set SECOND.

THE BACK To be Set FIRST.

USA; Complimentary calendar distributed by New Home Sewing machines, New Home manufacturers were located in Orange, Mass. at the time of this calendar, it is a color lithograph; on the back is the 1900 calendar; 10" across; $75.00.

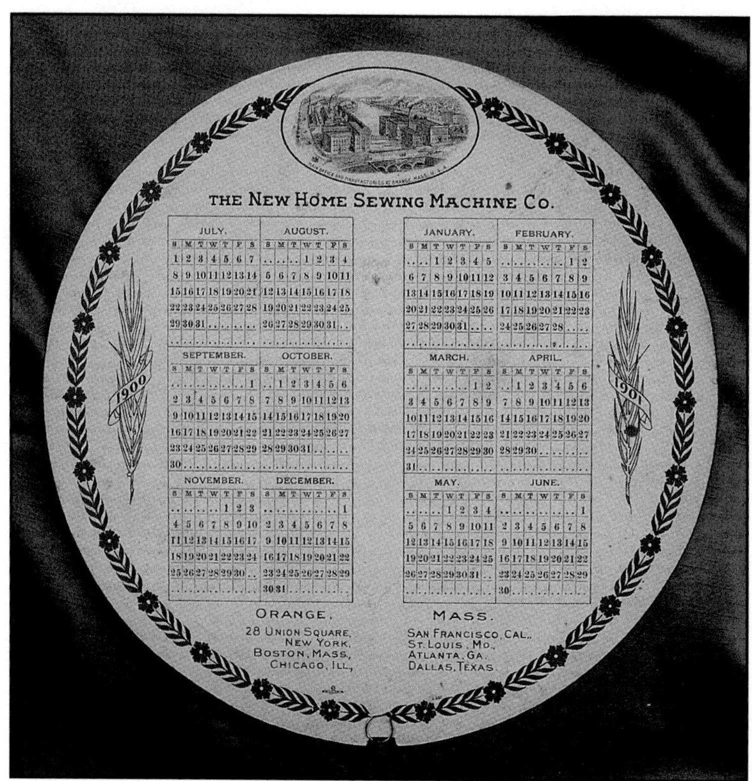

Windsor Prints ad, 1882.

NORTH ADAMS, JAN. 1882

·WINDSOR PRINTS·

UNUSUALLY LARGE COLLECTION
HIGH CLASS NOVELTIES FOR
THE SPRING SEASON OF
·1882·

NEWEST COLORINGS IN
CHOICEST PATTERNS.

ENCLOSED SAMPLES
JUST SENT OUT AND MAY
BE OBTAINED OF YOUR JOBBER
IF ORDERED AT ONCE.

·WINDSOR PRINTS·

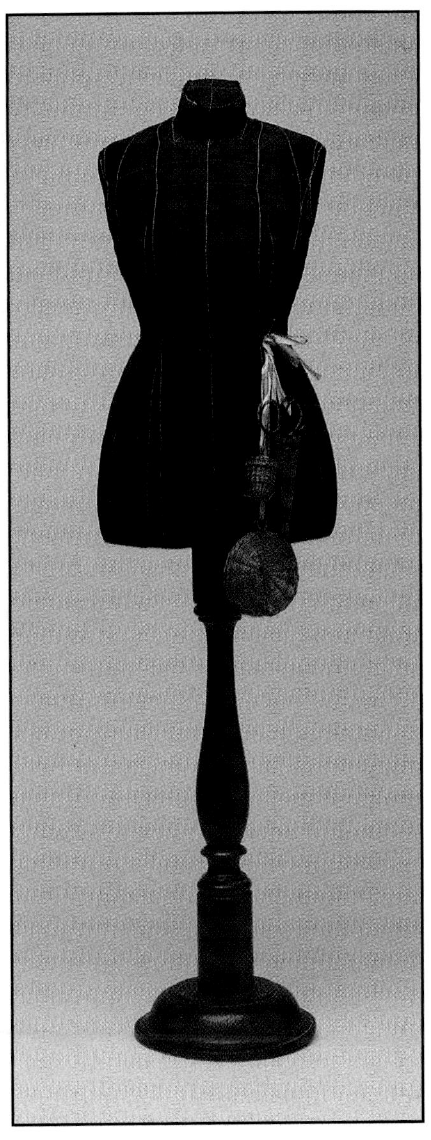

Italy; dressmaker's mannequin, wood stand, wool fabric cover with machine stitched pinning lines; c. 1900.
It has been said that samples of the latest fashion would be made and then the models would be displayed in the shop window, or possibly it was a mannequin for fashion dolls' clothing. Both suggestions would serve the same purpose, entice the women into having the newest style made up or purchase the fabric.
Pinned to the waist is a ribbon and sweet grass sewing chatelaine, pieces are scissors and sheath, pin and needle disc, and thimble holder with thimble; c. 1900. This item was a part of the Miriam Tuska Exhibit at the Museum of the American Quilter's Society in the fall of 1995, $350.00.

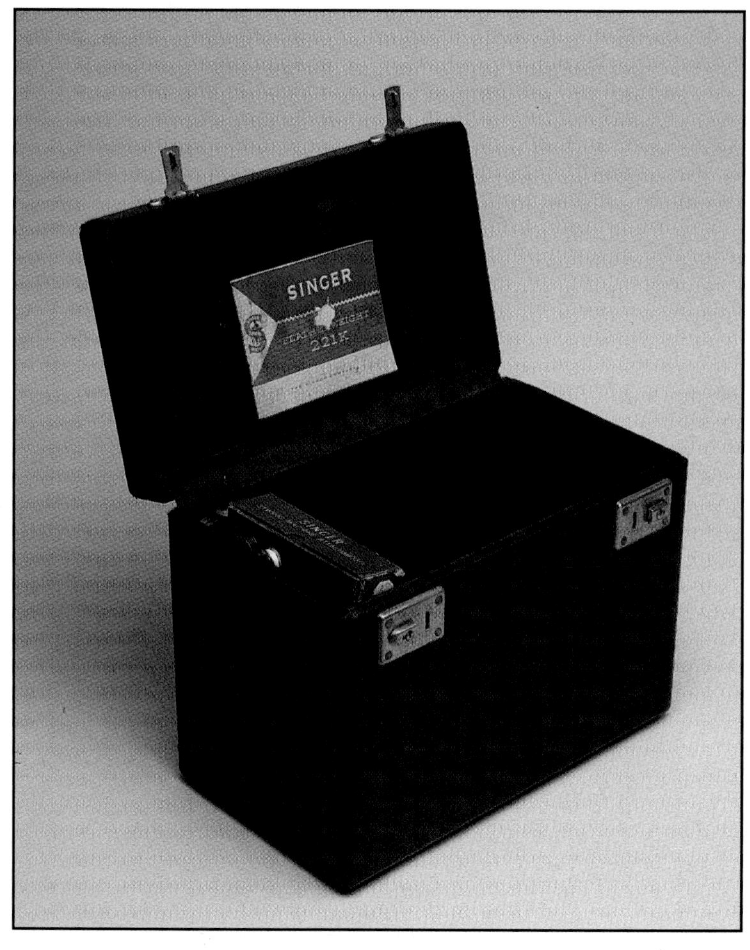

USA; Singer Featherweight Machine, cast metal, portable, simple gold design, complete with instruction book, full set of attachments, needles and bobbins; c. 1935, $400.00.

Carrying case is covered with treated fabric. There is space for the machine, foot pedal, attachments and other small items. Each closure has a lock. Each case has a storage tray, box, or lid clamp.

For an additional cost, a card table-style table with a cut-out to drop the machine in was available. When the table was not needed for sewing, the cut-out could be replaced and the table was useful for other activities. The table top was wood with metal trim and metal legs; $50.00–$100.00. There are reproductions of these tables being made by individuals.

The recent desirability of this particular Singer model is the result of the American quilt revival beginning in the 1970s. Their lightweight portable design and durable qualities are suitable for traveling to classroom situations for quiltmakers.

Front of framed "Improved Family Singer..." tradecard, 1884.

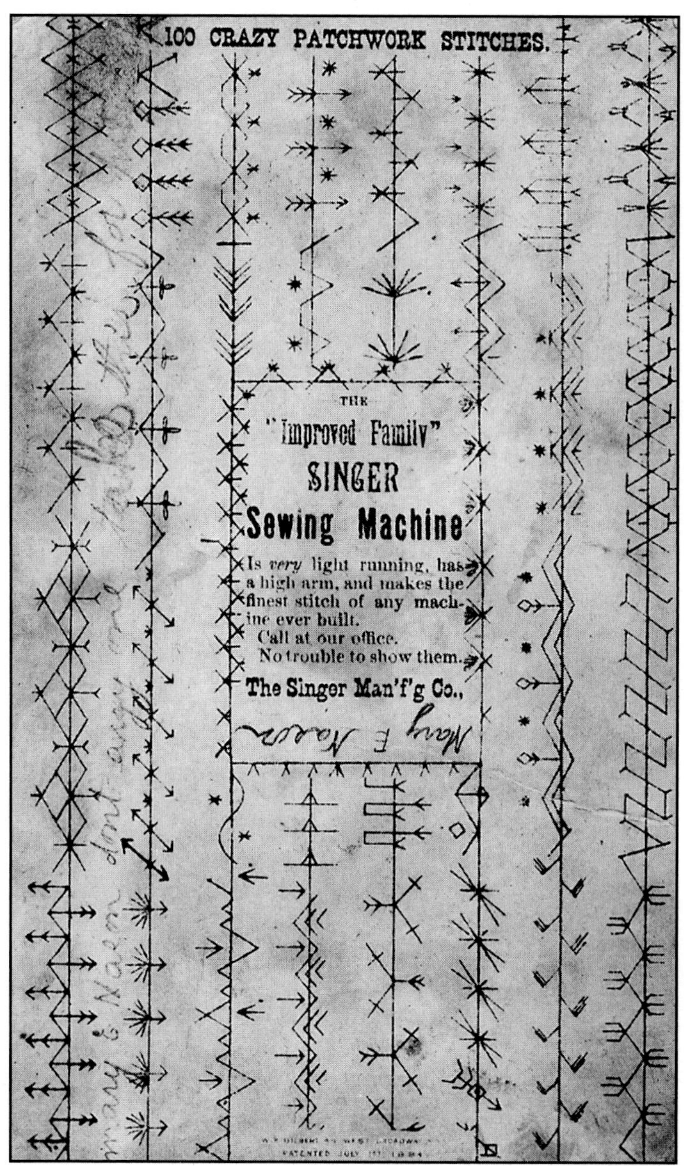

Back of framed "Improved Family Singer..." tradecard, 1884.

When he comes to your house...

he comes to *SERVE*

He is the authorized, bonded Representative of the Singer Sewing Machine Company—a world-wide organization of service to women who sew. He is one of 10,000 in the United States and Canada alone. But each is a *local* representative. The man who calls on you is a resident of your community. He is as much interested in serving you as your neighborhood banker or merchant. He is building a permanent business and he knows that one of his greatest assets is the good will of enthusiastic customers. Therefore his first concern always is to serve you honestly, faithfully and intelligently.

He has been carefully selected for his work. He has been trained by experts. When he comes to you he is qualified to discuss your needs and problems and to demonstrate to you the advantages, the enjoyment and the economies of the modern way to sew.

The modern Singer Electric has simply revolutionized sewing in the home. Once you sit down before it, once you feel its instant response to your slightest wish, you will realize that it is utterly different from any machine you have ever used. But you must make that test to know. And so the Singer man in your community comes to invite you to take any modern Singer into your home and use it without the slightest obligation. He comes to show you how you can find real enjoyment in planning and making clothes for yourself and the children and curtains and draperies for your home, how you can make a dress in a fraction of the time it used to take, how you can do quickly the deft finishing you thought must be done by hand. You will find that the magic means to this modern way to sew can be yours at surprisingly small cost. For the Singer man is authorized to make you a generous allowance on your present machine and arrange for the balance to be paid in small monthly sums which your Singer will save over and over again.

So if your home is one where the modern Singer Electric and the delights of modern sewing are not yet known, welcome the Singer man when he calls on you. His coming can mean the beginning of a new experience that you will enjoy and profit by all through life.

SINGER SEWING MACHINE COMPANY

SINGER ELECTRIC

Sewing *Machines*

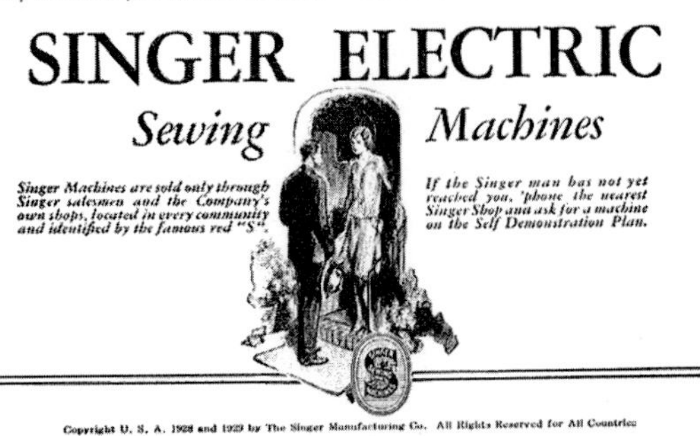

Singer Machines are sold only through Singer salesmen and the Company's own shops, located in every community and identified by the famous red "S".

If the Singer man has not yet reached you, 'phone the nearest Singer Shop and ask for a machine on the Self Demonstration Plan.

Needlecraft Magazine ad, 1929.

EARLY SPRING FASHIONS.

March, 1896.

THE YOUNG LADIES' JOURNAL

AN ILLUSTRATED MAGAZINE OF FASHION, FANCY WORK, FAMILY READING, ETC., ETC.

A New Story, ENTITLED 'A MARSH FAIRY' By Gertrude Warden, COMMENCES IN THIS PART.

Gratis Supplements:

A CUT-OUT Paper Pattern OF PELISSE FOR GIRL, From Five to Seven Years of Age.

AN ALBUM OF FASHIONS For LADIES & CHILDREN, Consisting of 8 Coloured Plates.

A Twelve Page Gigantic Supplement OF EARLY SPRING FASHIONS.

COLOURED SHEET: Fancy Pocket.

We do not employ *Travelling Agents* for our Cut-out Patterns or Subscriptions.

AMERICAN EDITION. Part 411. MARCH, 1896.

Published Wholesale by "THE INTERNATIONAL NEWS COMPANY," 83 & 85, Duane Street (one door east of Broadway), New York, and sold by all the NEWS COMPANIES and WHOLESALE AND RETAIL BOOKSELLERS THROUGHOUT THE UNITED STATES.—Price of Single Monthly Part,

The Young Ladies' Journal ad, March 1896.

The Young Ladies' Journal ad, March 1896.

Glossary

Bodkin: a blunt needle or flat tool with a long, slender eye for drawing ribbon, tape, or braid through casings or hems.

Brass: copper base alloy with zinc as the alloying agent.

Bronze: one of the earliest alloys made by man, in common use by 100 BC. It was used for tools as well as decorative items. Bronze is an alloy of copper, tin, and largely magnesium.

Celluloid: developed in 1856 from land plants, cotton, straw, jute, etc., a compound of cellulose nitrate and camphor. Manufactured in 1868 and often identified with novelty items and souvenirs.

Emboss: to adorn with raised decorative pattern. Pressure is applied against a steel die roll cut or engraved with a pattern.

Emery: a natural abrasive often used in powder form. It is used to fill small bags or shapes of natural items, such as a strawberry, sewn shut and used to remove rust from pins and needles as well as to sharpen the points.

Etui: French kit containing tools for sewing and/or personal use.

Filigree: ornamental, open work of a delicate intricate design.

Gold Fill: items made of a base metal overlaid with gold.

Jasperware: An unglazed vitreous fine stoneware. Mineral oxides are used to produce different colors. Wedgwood, the developer, has been in business since 1794.

Knitting: the creation of items by a series of intermeshing loops of yarn one row at a time using slender needles of varying sizes.

Lace: a patterned ornamental, open-work fabric.

Lady's Companion: a small carrying box of tools (see Necessaire).

Latten: an alloy of calamine, zinc carbonate, and copper resembling brass, hammered into thin sheets.

Lead: a bluish, white metallic element often used in combinations creating alloys.

Lusterware: earthenware decorated by applying to the glaze the metallic compounds which become iridescent metallic films when fired.

Mother-of-Pearl: a hard, pearly, iridescent inner layer of a fresh/or salt water mollusk shell, used for many different personal household and sewing items.

Necessaire: a small carrying case for small items, such as sewing, personal, and/or writing and drawing tools. They appeared in sales catalogs in the mid-1700s.

Nickel Plate: a thin layer of nickel joined by electrolysis to an object made of other metals to improve the finish and prevent rust.

Nickel Silver: a hard, tough alloy of nickel, copper, and zinc and is sometimes called "German silver."

Repousse: shaped or ornamented with patterns in relief made by hammering, or pressing on reverse side, used in metal work.

Tin: a lustrous low melting element that is used as a protective coating in tin foil, soft solder, and alloys.

Solder: an alloy of lead and tin used to join metal surfaces.

Stanhope: a very small glass rod about ¼" long that one can look through and see various magnified black and white scenes. The inventor was Charles Stanhope, 3rd Earl of Stanhope (1753 – 1816). Stanhope's were a decorative item in needlework tools from 1860 – 1915.

Stereograph: a picture composed of two superimposed stereoscopic images that gives a 3-D effect when viewed with a stereoscope.

Sterling: represents a standard of quality, 925 parts silver with 75 parts of copper. Abbreviations seen stamped on items are "ster.," "stg.," or "stig."

Vegetable Ivory: the corozo nut of a South American palm tree. The nut contains seeds that are the color and texture of ivory. When exposed to the light they turn a honey color. It is also called ivory nut and tagua nut. In use since 1700s by carvers and turners. The coquilla nut that comes from a Brazilian palm is about the size of a hen's egg. Because of its hardness, it has been popular with turners of small object since the 1500s. The shell of the coquilla was used to make small items, many of which were sewing items. The carving properties of both corozo and coquilla identify them with ivory.

Bibliography

Banister, Judith. ***English Silver Hallmarks***. London: W. Foulsham & Co. Ltd, 1900.

Cummins, Genevieve E. and Nerylla D. Tauton. ***Chatelaines, Utility to Glorious Extravagance.*** England: Antique Collectors' Club, 1994.

Encyclopedia Americana International Edition, The. Danbury, Connecticut: Grolier Incorporated 1991. Volume 16.

Encyclopedia Britannica. Volume 8, 1995.

Gerson, Roselyn. ***Vintage Vanity Bags and Purses.*** Paducah, KY: Collector Books, 1994.

Gullers, Barbara. ***Antique Sewing Tools and Tales***. United States and Sweden: 1992.

Houart, Victor. ***Sewing Accessories, an Illustrated History***. London: Souvenir Press Ltd., 1984.

Johnson, Eleanor. ***Needlework Tools, a Guide to Collecting***. England: Shire Publications Ltd., 1987.

Leopold, Allison Kyle. ***Cherished Objects. Living with and Collecting Victoriana***. USA: C. Potter Publishers, 1988.

Mathis, Averil. ***Antique & Collectible Thimbles and Accessories***. Paducah, KY: Collector Books, 1991

Muller, Wayne. ***Darn It! The History and Romance of Darners***. Indiana: L&W Book Sales, 1995.

Ormsbee, Thomas H. ***Field Guide to American Victorian Furniture***. New York, NY: Bonanza Books, 1953.

Pickford, Ian, ***Jackson's Hallmarks, Pocket Edition***. England: Antique Collectors' Club Ltd., 1993.

Rainwater, Dorothy T. ***Encyclopedia of American Silver Manufacturers***. Pennsylvania: Schiffer Publishing Ltd., 1986.

Rogers, Gay Ann. ***Illustrated History of Needlework Tools***. London: Johny Murray (Publishers) Ltd., 1989.

Thomas, Glenda. ***Toy and Miniature Sewing Machines***. Paducah, KY: Collector Books, 1995.

Wallace, Carol McD. ***Victorian Treasures, an Album and Historical Guide for Collectors***. New York, NY: Harry Abrams, Inc., 1993.

Warren, Geoffer. ***A Stitch in Time: Victorian and Edwardian Needlecraft***. England: David and James, 1976.

Webster's Seventh New Collegiate Dictionary. Springfield, Massachusetts: G & C Merriam Company, 1965.

Whiting, Gertrude. ***Tools and Toys of Stitchery***. New York, NY: Columbia University Press, 1928.

World Book Encyclopedia, The. Chicago: World Book, Inc. 1985. Volume 12.

Zalkin, Estelle. ***Thimble and Sewing Implements***. Pennsylvania: Warman Publishing Co., 1988.

Index